BEYOND

EMBRACING THE OUTWARD-FOCUSED HEART OF CHRIST

AN IGNITE MOVEMENT DEVOTIONAL

PRAYERSHOP
PUBLISHING

Terre Haute, Indiana

PrayerShop Publishing is the publishing arm of the Church Prayer Leaders Network. The Church Prayer Leaders Network exists to equip and inspire local churches and their prayer leaders in their desire to disciple their people in prayer and to become a "house of prayer for all nations." Its online store, prayershop.org, has more than 150 prayer resources available for purchase or download.

© 2023 Ignite Movement

ISBN (Print): 978-1-970176-21-6
ISBN (E-Book): 978-1-970176-22-3

CONTENTS

Part 4: Reaching Beyond to the Ends of the Earth

The Life That Has Been with Jesus

Imagine the impression a single day spent with Jesus during His earthly ministry would leave on your heart. As you wake up in the morning, the first thing you realize is that Jesus is missing. You start looking around and realize that Jesus awoke before sunrise and has wandered some distance to spend time alone with the Father and engage in His great work as an intercessor.

It's not long before streams of the poor, blind, demonized, women, children, and notorious sinners begin flocking to Jesus from all the surrounding villages. Not a single person is turned away. As many come to Him, He heals them. He touches the unclean, drives out demons, and dignifies each person as He looks into their eyes and restores their humanity.

Eventually, He motions for people to sit down and begins teaching the multitudes gathered around Him. You gaze across the sea of thousands of broken people, like lost sheep without a shepherd, and hear the words roll off His tongue, "Blessed are the poor in spirit, for theirs is the kingdom of heaven" (Matthew 5:3). On the margins of the crowd you see the religious elite murmuring and looking upon the hurting people with scorn. Jesus' whole ministry stands in contradistinction to their merciless hearts. Despite their sharp criticism,

He continues casting out devils, healing the sick, and proclaiming the Good News.

It's getting late in the day and you are getting tired. You and the other disciples haven't eaten all day, so you work up the courage to approach the Master, tap Him on the shoulder, and tell Him "perhaps it's time to dismiss the people, so they (and you) can go get something to eat." Jesus turns around and says, "You feed them." You immediately begin to calculate the improbability of what is being asked of you. You bring your objection to Jesus and He cooly responds, "bring me what you have."

He lifts His eyes to heaven to thank His Father for the meal as simply as if He had invited a few friends over for dinner. He breaks the bread and begins distributing it. Everyone eats until they have had their fill, and then you begin walking among the crowd to collect the leftovers.

Toward the Reoriented Life

One day spent with Jesus would completely reorient your life. His life of prayer, genuine compassion for people, mission to seek and save the lost, and intentionality in discipleship all powerfully reveal His outward-focused heart.

We believe that in this hour God is calling us to move *beyond* ourselves and embrace this same outward-focused heart. The harvest is plentiful, but the laborers are few. As we engage with Jesus' heart and pray for laborers to be raised up, we believe that we will inevitably become a part of the answer to those prayers.

God loves us, but He loves our neighbor too; therefore, He calls us *beyond* ourselves. "For Christ's love compels us, because we are convinced that one died for all, and therefore all died.

And he died for all, that those who live should no longer live for themselves but for him who died for them and was raised again"

(2 Corinthians 5:14-15). Christ's love compels us. It moves us from the inside out. The work Jesus performed in making us new creations and the example He set for us by laying His life down calls us to no longer live for ourselves.

As followers of Jesus, we have been caught up into a greater storyline. God is redeeming humanity and reconciling people to Himself and He has invited us to participate in this work. We get to bring the message of hope and restoration to a lost and broken world. As we demonstrate and carry the Good News of Jesus Christ to our cities, campuses and the nations of the world, we believe that the power of the Gospel will transform lives and entire communities.

Responding to the Invitation

During the Student Volunteer Missions Movement, the rallying cry wasn't "pray for us" or "support us" but "come with us." We believe that Jesus is standing in the harvest field of this generation and inviting us to come with Him. There is an intimacy we can only know with Jesus as we labor with Him in the harvest. It is in this place we witness His outward flowing heart toward humanity and get touched with the same passion. The devotions we have compiled in this book are designed to help you tap into that heart in Jesus and begin living from the inside out. Written by both seasoned and emerging voices within the Body of Christ, these devotionals come from those who are practicing the lifestyle of the "outward-focused heart of Christ" in their cities and communities.

How This Devotional Is Organized

There are four different sections to these daily devotions. The first section addresses the heart posture necessary to truly live from the inside out. The following three sections dive further into the specific mission fields of college campuses, cities, and the nations. The closing of this 21-day journey ends with a doxology (a song of praise), as we believe that the call of *beyond* is ultimately a call to worship. Each individual devotional begins with an anchor scripture and ends with a closing prayer. The firm witness of scripture, grounded in faithful and prayerful devotion is one of the most beautiful ways in which God transforms us from the inside out. That being said, our prayer is that you would engage with these two spiritual practices (scripture meditation and prayer) and as a result these devotions will pull you deeper into the missional heart of Jesus.

Start the Journey

We cannot take on this invitation to go *beyond* by ourselves. It can only be fully accomplished within the context of empowered communities who are practicing the way of Christ together. We encourage you to go through this devotional with your community—your family, friends, small group, and/or church.

Let's Go Beyond!

PART 1

A Heart that Reaches Beyond

"If I give all I possess to the poor and
give over my body to be burned, but
do not have love, I gain nothing."
1 Corinthians 13:3

These words spoken by Paul to the church of Corinth cause all
of our efforts to "change the world" to shrink into their proper
place, which are secondary to the first and foremost of all renewals:
the spiritual renewal of the heart and soul that produces a love that
comes only from Christ. This is an inward renewal that births and
sustains all real outward renewals.

Our good deeds and works will show up empty, without eternal
significance, when they are not built upon the foundation of Christ,
and Christ alone. Jesus likens those who build their lives upon anything other than Him to a man who builds his house upon sand only
to have it destroyed by rain, floods, and strong winds. One cannot live
the outward-focused *life* of Jesus without having the foundation of

the outward-focused *heart* of Jesus. The world-changing and eternally significant actions of Christ are inseparable to the heart of Christ.

Christian philosopher, Dallas Willard, says it this way: *"The revolution of Jesus is in the first place and continuously a revolution of the human heart and spirit."*

A heart that reaches beyond is a heart that is daily reaching for Jesus. He is the source of life, the only one who can restore our broken communities, rebuild our ruined cities, and revive our wayward hearts.

As we live with our hearts connected to Jesus, our way of life no longer moves under the direction of self, but it moves to His heartbeat. His conviction, His compassion, His faith, His action now become ours. He is the Lord of the Harvest who calls us to be with Him in the harvest field, and we must go beyond ourselves, with Him.

It is our desire that these devotions will take you into the beautiful heart and emotions of Jesus so that the outward-focused heart of Christ may be formed in greater ways in both your soul and actions.

Heart of Surrender

BY NIKO PEELE

*"We do not know what to do,
but our eyes are on you."*
2 Chronicles 20:12b

These were words spoken by King Jehoshaphat in the midst of battle as he and his army were surrounded by three armies plotting to destroy Judah. King Jehoshaphat was enclosed and seemingly out of options. There was only one direction he could take; he turned his face upward toward Heaven in surrender. At this moment, he gave up! He waved the white flag, except it wasn't to the armies that engulfed him, but to God. Through his confession and declaration of utter dependence on God, he made space for something beyond himself to fill his emptiness and empower him to do something he could not have done in his own strength. The very strength and empowering grace of God filled King Jehoshaphat. God gave clarity on what to do and Judah won a decisive victory.

The key to this victory was not in King Jehoshaphat's great training, skills, education, or anything related to his confidence and trust in himself or his own ability. It was the posture of his heart. He accessed the presence of God in the midst of battle through a posture of utter dependence and trust in God. He surrendered and God showed up.

Every day we are faced with our own challenges and battles. We may not be surrounded by physical armies trying to take our lives, but we are often surrounded by other enemies: fear, doubt, unbelief, insecurity, and other personal struggles. We may find ourselves overwhelmed by obligations, tasks, and responsibilities or maybe even by big dreams, God ideas, and aspirations to change the world. Whatever it may be, big or small, there is only one posture that can lead us to victory in Jesus Christ—a heart of surrender.

In Matthew 5, Jesus lays out the value system of the Kingdom of God in His famous Sermon on the Mount. He opens up His teaching with this statement:

"Blessed are the poor in spirit for theirs is the kingdom of Heaven." (v. 3)

The Kingdom of Heaven (all of the realities of Heaven above, made real and tangible, in the here and now) is advanced in our contexts not through the spiritually proud but through the spiritually humble, the ones who have plenty of space for God to fill and empower by His Spirit. The Sermon on the Mount continues with many more values of the Kingdom, but it's important to note that it begins with what must come first and remain central—surrender.

Those who God empowers to advance His Kingdom-work, from heaven to earth, are those who have embraced a heart posture of surrender. They are the ones who are aware and acknowledge their deep need for God that draws Him near to show up in every area of their lives. Practically, for King Jehoshaphat this looked like (1) acknowledging his inability to bring victory in his own strength ("We do not know what to do") and (2) taking his eyes off of himself and placing the situation unto God—the only one who could bring victory (". . . but our eyes are on you"). These two practical decisions (acknowledging his need for God and shifting his gaze) welcomed God.

This theme of surrender is echoed all throughout scripture and in each instance it reveals how a heart posture of surrender always invokes God's living presence into our lives and into our situations. Reflect on these scriptures and allow the Holy Spirit to draw your heart into deeper intimacy with God.

> "For this is what the high and exalted One says—he who lives forever, whose name is holy: 'I live in a high and holy place, but also with the one who is contrite and lowly in spirit, to revive the spirit of the lowly and to revive the heart of the contrite.'" (Isaiah 57:15)

> "I, the LORD, have spoken! 'I will bless those who have humble and contrite hearts, who tremble at my word.'" (Isaiah 66:2 NLT)

> "For whoever would save his life will lose it, but whoever loses his life for my sake will find it." (Matthew 16:25 ESV)

> "Draw near to God and He will draw near to you . . ." (James 4:8 NKJV)

The late Andrew Murray says, "Just as water seeks and fills the lowest place, so the moment God finds you abased and empty, His glory and power flow in."

No matter what season of life we are in, whether we feel helpless or we feel empowered, when we bow low in humility and surrender we welcome the glorious leadership of God to rush in like a river in and through us. This is how we walk in our original design and purpose. This is how we overcome like King Jehoshaphat. This is how we are compelled to love sacrificially the poor, the orphan, the persecuted, and even our enemies. This is how we live BEYOND, with the outward-focused heart of Jesus pulsating within us. Desperate surrender for God Himself is the welcome mat for the reign of His kingdom in our lives.

Prayer:

Jesus, help me to never outgrow my awareness of my need for You. May I never graduate from utter dependance on You. May I always lay before You as an empty vessel, in surrender, for the purpose of Your heart alone to fill. Give me a heart of surrender, so I may see Your Kingdom come, and Your will be done in our world.

Niko Peele is the founder and director of Ignite Movement.

Heart of Compassion

BY DAR DRAPER

"Ask and it will be given to you; seek and you will
find; knock and the door will be opened to you."
Matthew 7:7

I was never much of a crier, but I have always been a dreamer. One
day, after experiencing a season of spiritual stirring along with a
bit of what I call "divine dissatisfaction," I prayed this prayer: "Lord,
give me more of a heart for kids in the world!"

I profoundly heard that still small voice answer, "Ok . . . but
you'll cry a lot."

I found that response curious, as I associated tears of that variety
as belonging to deeply compassionate people. I was always in pursuit
of "an increased capacity to love," and had discovered that loving
God and people was my greatest call. However, true *compassion* felt
beyond my wheelhouse. This prayer for children in the world served
as my invitation to the biggest and messiest renovation project I had
ever encountered: the renovation of my heart.

Not too many weeks later, an opportunity came and I was asked to host an orphan from Ukraine for four weeks around Christmas time. I didn't want to. I had a myriad of "legitimate excuses," but my husband and I were children's pastors . . . Could I say there was no room at the inn? And I had just prayed this prayer . . . and the world came knocking. We said "yes," and the renovation project of my heart began.

About one week after 16-year-old Sasha arrived, the tears started. The gravity of what it means to be an orphan hit me. "This kid has no parents!" I lamented within. I had worked with kids my whole adult life, and never really considered the orphan. "Who is going to teach him right from wrong? Who is going to be there for him in life?" I couldn't imagine my kids truly alone without an advocate in this life who LOVED them.

This "imagining" was the beginning of the work that dug the well of compassion in my soul—a new kind of love that fueled action. After the hosting period, we had to send Sasha back to his orphanage in Ukraine, but God continued to stir us and stretch us. After the second hosting that summer, we had to go. Sasha could not be adopted, but he had become our son and we wanted an introduction to his world. So, we went in September of 2016. We met his friends, and loved them too. We learned of the orphan crisis and what happens to aged-out orphans. The statistics are staggering; high prostitution, incarceration and suicide rates, and the worst is that the average life expectancy of an aged-out orphan is 30 years old!

After learning this, we had to do something. We couldn't just let them fall prey to these statistics at the hands of a society with a stigma against orphans. We continued going and planned a camp and graduation project for Sasha's class. Our plans and efforts seemed simple to us, yet extravagant to them. When we came to the orphanage, workers often made comments like, "Why do you do all this for them? They are just orphans." Just orphans . . .

After this camp, my third trip to Ukraine, my husband and I saw so much life-changing fruit that we just had to do more. We prayed about quitting our 10-year positions as full-time children's pastors and starting our own ministry to the children of the world. The Lord confirmed our decision to take this next leap in a curious way. He reminded me of a moment I had while snorkeling on an anniversary trip ten years prior. I was overwhelmed by the brilliance of underwater life, the vibrant colors of the tropical fish and plant life! I got teary in my mask, praising God for His outstanding creativity! Then I spotted this ONE fish . . . looking at me. We stared at each other until he darted away. The thought occurred, *What if I was the only one on the planet who ever got to see that fish?* As we prayed about giving our life to care for these kids, God asked, "What if you are the ONLY ONE who will ever see their beauty and what I deposited in them?" I had to go and let them know.

Our initial "yes" turned into a complete change of path forged by many, many tears. Now a well of compassion continues to fuel our mission. How grateful I am that He responded to my simple prayer and that Jesus is still about His Father's business of building and renovating hearts.

Prayer:

Lord, increase my capacity to love. Renovate my heart and make my life a space where others encounter Your great love. May Your compassion for Your kids well up within me and fuel my mission, Your Great Commission, and may my life be used to bring Your kids back to You. Amen.

Dar Draper is the co-founder and executive director of GLOW Mission.

Heart of Conviction

BY DAVID AND JASON BENHAM

"Whoever believes in me, as Scripture has said,
rivers of living water will flow from within them."
John 7:38

Leonard Ravenhill once said, "The world out there is not waiting for a new definition of Christianity; it's waiting for a new demonstration of Christianity."

How true this is.

At a time in history when Christians have more resources than ever before—more conferences, more influencers, more technology, you name it—our culture continues to slide morally and spiritually while Christian influence drifts to the background.

Bigger buildings and cooler conferences clearly have not produced the spiritual transformation our nation desperately needs.

So what are we to do?

Start living from the inside out, as convictional (not cultural) Christians once again. Slowly, generationally, our lives will begin to refresh those around us with the river of Living Water (John 7:38).

It's time to be fountains, not drains.

Think about a water fountain. When you are thirsty and press the button, what comes out? Water—nourishment for your body. For a fountain to give nourishment, it has to be connected to a source. If not, you can press the button all day, but nothing will come out. There's nothing inside the fountain to satisfy your thirst.

Likewise, if we do not connect to God as our Life Source, when our "button is pressed," nothing comes out to nourish others (John 15:4–5). But when we do connect, divine life will flow through us.

Transformation begins with us. This is what it means to be a convictional Christian—to live from the inside out.

We must develop the inner person before we develop outer disciplines and before we try to transform the world. Otherwise, our disciplines become religious burdens and we become a horde of noisy radicals with lots of ideas and no real substance (think definition more than demonstration). But when we connect to Christ and live from the inside out, disciplines become our joy, and changing our world becomes natural.

God always works from the inside out—from the heart of man to the heart of culture. So as we develop our internal life in Christ, we will also develop the spiritual resources to live with dignity and to act with power when the tide of culture pushes against us.

In our own lives, we focus on five core areas of conviction as we examine our own faith (2 Corinthians 13:5):

- Do we know God . . . intimately, relationally, no secrets, full surrender?
- Do we know who God made us to be . . . in Him, as believers, using *our* uniqueness to show *His*?
- Do we think like children of God . . . submitted to Scripture and the local Church?
- Do we live by a biblical worldview . . . in our relationships, finances, and our work?

- Do we live reverently before the Lord . . . seeking to stand for truth no matter the cost?

As we ponder these questions and answer them as honestly as we can, we find that God often brings course correction in our lives and then uses us to impact others because we're living convictional not culturally. God takes our mess and makes it a message, a nourishing stream of water.

This world doesn't need a new definition of Christianity—it needs a new demonstration of it. Let that begin with us.

Prayer:

Jesus, strip us of cultural Christianity. We want to know You as the Fountain of Life, from where our soul drinks. Convict me with Your love so that I will live from Your love and be a living demonstration of Christ to my culture and those around me.

David and Jason Benham are best-selling authors and entrepreneurs.

Heart of Faith

BY PAUL HUGHES

*"And what more shall I say? I do not have
time to tell about Gideon . . . whose weakness
was turned to strength; and who became
powerful in battle and routed foreign armies."*
Hebrews 11:32–34

Hebrews chapter 11 is sometimes called "the Hall of Faith." The writer gives followers of Jesus examples of ordinary people in the Old Testament who by faith accomplished the impossible or unimaginable.

Those familiar with the story of Gideon in Judges chapters 6 and 7, may be surprised to find him in the Hebrews 11 list with Samson, David, and Samuel. Wasn't Gideon the second guesser? Didn't he question the authenticity of the angel who visited him and called him to become a leader in Israel? Didn't he object to God's choice of HIM with excuses of how small and insignificant he and his family and clan were? Didn't Gideon choose to destroy the altars of Baal and Asherah in secret during the night for fear of retaliation from his village?

Yes. Gideon was a fearful, insecure man living in a fearful, insecure generation.

But that is why the story of how Gideon went from a coward hiding in a winepress to become a powerful deliverer for his nation is a story we all can embrace. If God were to show up in your life today and call you to something far beyond what you could imagine, how would *you* respond?

Guess what? If you have said "yes" to the gospel call of Jesus to lay down your life, pick up your cross, and follow Him, that means you have *already* been chosen to accomplish impossible things for Him by faith! Let's look at Gideon for inspiration.

Becoming the Person God Chooses

Take time to read Judges chapters 6 and 7. I know reading some chapters of the Bible can be challenging, but this story moves! It will not bore you. As you read, notice the stages that Gideon goes through. Is there anything that surprises you about how God patiently works with Gideon?

Compare Gideon in 6:11-16 with Gideon in 7:13-15. In 6:16, the promise of God is "I will be with you and you will strike down all the Midianites together." In 7:15, Gideon has come to a full assurance of faith that the promise of God to defeat the vast Midianite army will come to pass with only 300 Israelite soldiers! What a transformation!

Examine the passage to see what God uses to build faith in Gideon's heart as a leader. What role do angels, signs, dreams, dream interpretation, and hearing the voice of the Lord directly play in this process of producing both belief that God will do what He said and the trust to risk everything to see it happen?

There are many lessons in Judges 6 and 7 one can learn about
how God works in the lives of those He chooses. I want to focus on
the paradox of how God's strength is made perfect in our weakness.
This truth is consistent throughout the Bible. The new covenant
apostle Paul said that he had been given "a thorn in his flesh" which
was a reminder to not trust his own strength, but God's (see 2 Corinthians 12). This is not always easy to do because we are prone to
pride. God has indeed chosen us and spoken to us. We are also prone
to fear because we look at our own weakness and lose hope that we
can survive or fulfill what God is calling us into. No doubt, we *would*
fail, if it were not for the most important part of the promise of God.

"I will be with you."

It is the promise of God's presence with us that produces the faith
we need to act on God-sized words. It is also the promise of God's
presence with us that produces the trust we rest in that God will
accomplish His purposes through our weakness. Indeed, God is well
able to work in spite of our efforts to accomplish what He desires!
That is good news! Faith in God is different from performing flaw-
lessly! Our confidence is in *His* ability to take our sometimes fragile
"yes" and bring great glory to Himself, or great blessing to others.

This came home to me one evening when I was about to speak
at a Christian fellowship at Florida State University more than 20
years ago. I had prepared a message, but I really wasn't confident in
what I had prepared. Honestly, this was not unusual. I was rarely the
kind of public speaker who brimmed with confidence. There was an
inward struggle happening as I sat on the front row about to offer
what I knew would surely be a lame message that no would like.
Pride comes in different packages. For sure, I was afraid to fail and
be embarrassed. But I was more afraid of the opinions of the people
in the room, than I was of not speaking a word in season from the
Spirit of God to His needy people. The voice of the Lord broke into
my internal dialog.

"Paul, you are too strong for me to use you tonight."

It wasn't the angel of the Lord appearing to Gideon, but the internal voice of God had the same impact. Notice, God didn't say, "Paul, you are too weak for me to use you tonight." That was actually what I already believed! Like Gideon, in my version of fear, false humility, and insecurity, I had decided something about who God used and didn't use. I was immediately genuinely grieved by my pride and self-absorption. And I was strengthened for the task for which I was called to speak. I repented of caring what others thought and trusted the Holy Spirit to give me words that would be a blessing to those listening.

When we look at the story of Gideon, it would be easy to think that the main point of the story is about the transformation of a man from fear to faith. While that is true, it leaves out the crisis of the hour and the need of the nation for God's supremacy to once again be put on display before the whole world. I believe we are living in an historic cultural crisis, needing a new generation of deliverers to become courageous voices for heavenly breakthrough.

My prayer for you, and for me, is that the One True and Living God will find us, wherever we may be hiding, and equip us with faith to wage the Gospel of peace on the antichrist armies terrorizing our world in this age.

Prayer:

Father, forgive me for making everything about myself, instead of Your purposes. Raise me up to be confident in Your strength to do all that You have promised through the ages. Give me the words and strategies of Heaven. Send angels to assist the saints in the land. Raise up an army of lovesick warriors! Father, I pray that Jesus, the Desire of the Nations, the apple of Your eye, the Lord of the Universe and Hope of the World, would so grip the Church in this hour that we would grow in love and faith to act valiantly and violently in the weapons of Your Spirit. This is not a generation of faint hearts, but faithful hearts! For Your eternal glory I pray. Amen."

Paul Hughes is the president of Kingdom Forerunners and campus director of Ignite at the University of Alabama-Birmingham.

Heart of Action

BY YASMINE PEIRCE

"Village life ceased, it ceased in Israel, until
I, Deborah, arose, a mother in Israel."
Judges 5:7 NKJV

We can look all around us and see signs of "village life" ceasing. Most of us probably do not need to look very far into today's society to see brokenness and the need of a Savior. In Deborah's time, Israel underwent 20 years of oppression from an invading army. This meant 20 years where fear and hopelessness ruled the streets. Even the bravest soldiers failed to stand up against the enemy. Imagine a once vibrant village life, drastically changing to darkness and an inability to even go outside and walk the streets safely, due to the infiltration of an enemy.

The truth is, whether that's our literal reality or not, this is the spiritual reality all around us today as a result of the fall. When Adam and Eve chose to step outside of the perfect will of the Father, they introduced sin and separation from God to all of humanity. Today, there is an enemy parading throughout our streets and you can see it in the form of the depression, loneliness, and hopelessness in our schools, our workplaces, our cities, and even our own families. Village life has ceased.

The reality, however, is that Jesus Christ has already won the victory. Similar to Deborah's day, God already had the victory against Israel's enemies in his hand. Jesus holds the keys of death and the grave because of His death and resurrection. He has called us to join in on the mandate of setting captives free. As we learn in 2 Corinthians 5, we are ambassadors for Christ.

The gap between the state of our campuses, workplaces and cities and the promise that Christ makes available is the heart of action for the Christian. Deborah was not the most courageous warrior of her day. She was a judge, but you do not even hear of an extravagant courthouse and riches. She simply sat under a tree to hold her meetings. But there, she also met with God.

It is in this place of meeting with God that our simple hearts get set on fire for the needs around us. God made it clear to Deborah that He knew the terrible situation that her nation was in, and He gave her instructions to secure the victory. A heart that is in friendship with God will gain His compassion for the world around us. Not only that, it will gain faith that He can do the impossible through us.

What is so interesting in this verse in Judges 5 is that Deborah does not choose to call herself a judge. She could have used her governmental authority to say that she was the right person to rise up. She could have also called herself a prophetess—a woman used by God. She did not choose either of these terms, but she chose the role of a mother as her most significant identity. What is even more interesting is the fact that we don't even know from the Bible if Deborah had children—she may not even biologically have been a mother! But the distinction here is that she had the heart of a mother.

In 1 Corinthians, Paul encourages the Church that they have many instructors, but not many fathers. Whether we are young or old, with children or not, God invites us to a place where we share the heart of a father—or mother—that would absolutely compel us into action for our generation. This is the adoptive heart, which says "I will take on your burden with you, and help you to see break through."

What would happen if this generation of leaders were not just good speakers and teachers, but we had the heart of mothers and fathers that deeply loved the people around us. This is the heart of action. Jesus invites us to be utterly driven by His own love.

Prayer:

God, we can see that village life has ceased all around us! But we know that this is not a reason to give up hope, it is a reason to draw ever closer to You in friendship. You are the miracle working God, and You have already secured the victory! Pour out Your love into my heart by the power of the Holy Spirit! May my life embody the heart of action, to lead this generation to the salvation and love of Christ!

Yasmine Peirce is a preacher and leader within Circuit Riders and Black Voices Movement

PART 2

Reaching Beyond for Campus Renewal

There are currently around 20 million students enrolled in colleges and universities in the United States alone and over 200 million globally. Estimates state that the average college campus in the U.S. is around 5% reached for the Gospel and nearly 70% of students who enter as believers will graduate with little or no faith. However, college campuses have also served as historic seedbeds of awakenings and missions movements. So how are we to honestly look at this population of cultural architects and future leaders in society?

Jesus gives us a way to look *beyond* in Matthew 9:36-38—through the lenses of compassion and faith. When Jesus saw the sea of people stretched out before Him, "*He was moved with compassion.*" He felt their brokenness at the gut level. He saw that they were like sheep without a shepherd, like orphans without fathers, and that they were spiritually confused and helpless. They were a broken generation. However, Jesus also said while looking upon the same mass of people, "*the harvest is plentiful.*" When our hearts are moved with compassion and filled with faith, we are given the ability to look *beyond* what we see in the natural and imagine God's better narrative for college students.

Andy Byrd from Youth With a Mission has said that "There are enough statistics to show that Gen Z could easily be the most missional and evangelistically inclined generation in history. . . . We are absolutely postured for one of the greatest waves of Jesus the Evangelist rising in the nations again and Jesus the Missionary arising. I believe this generation is pre-wired to tap into that heart in Jesus as the evangelist and the missionary to not only see the 3.2 billion people around the world who are still waiting for the reaching of the Gospel, but also to believe for the re-evangelization of our own nation."

We believe that God wants to visit college and university campuses with historic revival and an outpouring of His Spirit in such a way that will bring awakening to our nation. We believe that what God did in the Student Volunteer Missions Movement He can do again! We believe that God can send another wave of the Jesus People Movement that will once again contend with the secular narrative and rewrite headlines. We believe that Jesus will ultimately be glorified on college campuses.

Bill Bright, the founder of Campus Crusade for Christ (now CRU), once said that "If we can win the university today, we will win the world tomorrow." Whether you are currently a university student, mother or father, pastor, or someone who is simply concerned about future generations, we must all get beyond ourselves and embrace the outward focused heart of Christ to see this generation transformed by the power of the Gospel. We must pray for laborers, intercede for the lost, share the Gospel with boldness, strategize and collaborate to see every campus reached, and consider what the Lord may be asking of us.

College campuses are a place in our cities where the harvest is truly plentiful. We hope that the following devotions will stir your heart to contend for this generation and the mission field of college campuses.

DAY 6

Life in Community

BY LUKE TAYLOR

"Always be humble and gentle. Be patient
with each other, making allowance for
each other's faults because of your love."
Ephesians 4:2 NLT

Christopher McCandless had just received his college degree.
With job opportunities lined up and the American Dream of
money, success, and opportunity right before his eyes he disappeared.
Prior to his disappearance, McCandless grew apathetic toward this
American dream of success and believed life was more than mere
accomplishments. The next several years of his life would be a solo
journey of searching for the quintessential point of life.

McCandless was devoutly committed to a certain philosophy: it
was better for man to be alone. Tired of disappointments, McCandless figured there could be no let-down if no one existed to let him
down. Have you ever identified with McCandless' experience of
community? Perhaps this is your very feeling as you read this. If so,
know that your feelings are probably valid.

When I first began dating my wife, we constantly returned to a certain scripture that anchored our relationship in the truth of God's love:

"Always be humble and gentle. Be patient with each other, making allowance for each other's faults because of your love." (Ephesians 4:2 NLT)

There are many beautiful truths that shine in this scripture. Can I tell you my favorite? People are going to fail you. You are going to fail them. None of us are perfect. Yet, despite this reality, Paul tells us to "make allowance for each other's faults because of your love." The hardest thing I've ever done in my life has been marrying my wife. It is also the greatest accomplishment and joy of my life. Despite this reality, marriage is still hard at times. The reason? Because marriage is about death and new life. Two people becoming one flesh means many things, and one of those is that half of each other must die so something new and beautiful can be born. My wife and I quickly learned the only way we would be able to make our marriage work was to realize we needed to offer each other grace and make allowance for the times we would fail each other.

Grace is beautiful, isn't it? Grace is the essence of making allowance for each other's faults when we don't deserve it.

Deitrich Bonhoeffer was a brilliant theologian and leader in the Body of Christ. God placed his life on earth during the treacherous reign of Adolf Hitler and the Holocaust. Fueled by conviction and his love for the Gospel, Bonhoeffer resisted Hitler and Nazi ideology to eradicate Jews. He would ultimately lose his life due to this resistance and was executed by the Nazis on April 9, 1945, at the age of 39.

His final words were: "This may be the end—for me, the beginning of life." Although Bonhoeffer was taken from this world too soon, his life is a reminder of what surrender to the Lord looks like. Bonhoeffer's most notable work comes from a term he coined "Cheap Grace":

> "Cheap grace is grace without discipleship, grace without the cross, grace without Jesus Christ."

While grace is a gift worth receiving, it is never a gift worth abusing. Community is impossible without grace. It is also impossible with cheap grace. My wife and I realized something I believe changed the trajectory of our marriage. The grace we offer in making allowances for each other's faults is not a license to continue doing the same thing, but an empowerment which would allow this grace to change us from the inside out.

You may read this and think to yourself, *that's great and all, but I'm not currently married—what does all this have to do with my life in community?* Everything.

Marriage is a beautiful metaphor demonstrating how God chooses to spiritually form us into the man or woman He originally designed us to become, but so is community.

Jesus once said,

> "Love one another. As I have loved you, so you must love one another. By this everyone will know that you are my disciples, if you love one another." (John 13:34-35)

You and I were made for community. Even when it's hard, undesirable, scary, annoying, and negative emotions result from interactions we've had with others, the truth remains we were made for community. It's time we learn what true grace is and how we offer it to each other in the context of community. It's time we learn how to love one another the way Jesus loves us.

Remember that guy Christopher McCandless? Sadly, like Bonhoeffer, his life ended far too early. His body was discovered in the Alaskan wilderness in an abandoned bus which became his shelter during the winter season. However, the last thing he ever wrote in his journal tells us everything we need to know about a revelation that would have changed the trajectory of his life: "Happiness is only real, when shared."

Prayer:

Father, thank You for giving me a vision for what community can look like. Though it isn't perfect, I thank You for Your grace that reminds me that I can make allowance for other's faults as they do the same for me. Give me the grace today to love others as You first loved me. Amen.

Luke Taylor is the lead and founding pastor of Selah Church and national team member of Ignite Movement.

Disciple-Making Movements

BY STEVE SHADRACH

"But as for you, Timothy . . ."
2 Timothy 2:1

The 65-year-old Apostle Paul knew he was about to be put to death and was struggling. Not because he was afraid of Emperor Nero or of dying, but laying in that cold, dark Roman jail he was questioning whether his lifetime of sacrifice really amounted to anything. He decided to write a second and final letter to Timothy, a young disciple he'd mentored for 17 years, to pour out his thoughts and emotions:

". . . night and day I constantly remember you in my prayers. . . . I long to see you, so that I may be filled with joy." (2 Timothy 1:3-4)

". . . everyone in the province of Asia has deserted me." (2 Timothy 1:15)

A battle was going on in Paul's mind between faith and despair. All alone, cut off from any of the churches he had planted, and getting reports of spiritual betrayals and enemies everywhere, he wondered, *Was my life and ministry all in vain? Will the work continue? How will the gospel spread? Will the fragile young movement die out? Who can I pass the baton of leadership to?*

He realized the answer to those questions would not be found in a program or a quick fix, but in a man—his key man—Timothy, who was a 35-year-old single pastor in big, bad Ephesus, who was being attacked from without and within.

Paul could have injected pessimism and hopelessness into his timid disciple or challenge him to step up and walk toward his fears. He was thinking: *Even though it may appear everything is crumbling around us, Timothy, I have some final exhortations for you. The only way you are going to be able to grow and multiply this movement is if you totally commit to these principles. , , , But as for you, Timothy:*

"Be strong in the grace that is in Christ Jesus." (2 Timothy 2:1)

"And the things you have heard me say in the presence of many witnesses entrust to reliable people who will also be qualified to teach others." (2 Timothy 2:2)

"Join with me in suffering, like a good soldier of Christ Jesus." (2 Timothy 2:3)

In spite of all the confusion and opposition, Timothy was to be different by fully leaning upon the loving arms of Jesus through thick and thin. He was to remember the years of teaching and training he received from Paul and pass it on to others; but not just anybody. No, he was to be very picky as to *whom* he invested himself. That word "entrust" is a banking term in the Greek language. He was to take the precious and invaluable Christian faith and ministry Paul had patiently deposited into his life, and find faithful men to dial and open the combination lock of their hearts to place this eternal message into.

Paul wanted the chain to continue unbroken by these third generation disciples (1st Paul, 2nd Timothy, 3rd "faithful" ones) who were then to multiply themselves into fourth generation ("others") all over the world. Person to person disciple making was the secret key to sustain and multiply this movement in generations to come.

Lastly, Paul was trying to stiffen the spine of young Timothy who was allowing fear to grip him. He should welcome suffering, not run from it. He should seek to be a good soldier in God's army. This word "soldier" in the original language is *strata logos*—or "a word about strategy." The kind of warrior Paul was seeking to leave behind to multiply his legacy was one who had a specific strategy to fulfill the Great Commission.

Christians seem to have well thought out strategies in dating, study and grades, fitness, entrepreneurial and financial growth, even how to grow their social media followers (!) . . . but seldom do I see one with any kind of real strategy to win and disciple others for the Lord. But to be a good soldier in Christ Jesus, we must be willing to make tremendous sacrifices to craft and pursue a plan to reach the world for Christ through making disciples. And to do so, Paul is telling us, you must provide the necessary affection and direction to your young converts if you hope to have them live out their lives for the person and purpose of Jesus Christ.

Prayer:

Lord, do not let me be controlled by the threats and temptations swirling around me, but depend every moment on Your amazing strength and grace. Help me to look to You as my Commanding Officer, taking my marching orders from You, and You alone. God, I want to leave a legacy like Paul did; one that will outlive me and bring honor and glory to You. I know I need a Paul in my life to continue to train and equip me. Show me the right person to approach to play that role for me. And Father, I want to make a difference in this world with my life. Give me a great strategy and discernment as to which individuals I can start to pray for, witness, win to Christ, and disciple. I want to selflessly pour myself into these growing Christians so that they, in turn, can multiply their lives into others. Oh Lord, don't let me be the last link in this chain. In Jesus name. Amen

Steve Shadrach is an author, speaker and global ambassador for the Center for Missions Mobilization.

Prayer for Historic Revival on Campus

BY CHIS NGAI

". . . how much more will your heavenly Father give the Holy Spirit to those who ask and continue to ask Him!"
Luke 11:13 AMP

History was never meant to be forgotten or left behind us; it was meant to call us to something more. The testimonies of God are meant to connect us with the storyline of heaven and to reveal how much less we've settled for in our present-day reality. They are meant to birth a heart-cry within us that can never be satisfied until we see Him move again!

The stories of God create:

- Faith within our hearts to believe for more.
- Hope within us that dares to dream with Him.
- Holy jealousy that provokes us to pray like we've never prayed before!

God has called our generation to be one that makes history—that opens the door for the King of Glory to enter in (Psalm 24)! In order to do this, we must embrace our identity as a generation that seeks His face, as one who will pray until He comes.

1. If we want to make history, we must dream the kinds of dreams that change history. A young man named Evan Roberts was consumed with a desire for revival in his generation. He believed and dreamed with God for 10 years, praying for an outpouring of the Holy Spirit. When the revival came to Wales in 1904, more than 100,000 people came to Christ in less than a year, and a great transformation took place throughout Wales.

2. If we want to make history, we must pray the kinds of prayers that change history. In 1967, an Asbury student named Jeannine Brabon was consumed with a desire for revival on her campus! She would pray all hours of the day for a move of God. Then she gathered a small group of students to pray with her before each chapel service. In October 1969, an all-night prayer meeting unexpectedly brought 150 students into a powerful encounter with God's presence.

   In February 1970, when revival broke out in Asbury's chapel service, students flooded the altar to pray, pour out their souls, to repent and call out to God! Testimonies and open confession of sin began to pour forth publicly. Classes were canceled, as students and faculty continued to experience the presence of God 24-hours-a-day for the next seven days. Out of this heaven-sent revival, more than 130 schools were impacted throughout the nation and thousands made decisions for Christ as a result. Wherever these students shared the testimony, revival would break out on campuses, in churches and communities.

3. If we want to make history, we must be willing to become the answers to history-changing prayer. In 1806, five college students were caught in a thunderstorm while discussing the great need for missions. They took refuge in a nearby haystack. As they counted the cost of giving everything for the sake of the gospel among the nations, objection after objection arose, until one of the young men, Samuel Mills, boldly declared: "We can do it, if we will!" This led to what became known as the Haystack Prayer Meeting, which gave birth to student missions in America. This would lay the groundwork for the Student Volunteer Movement 80 years later, which would send forth 20,000 students into the nations of the earth. The rallying cry of that movement became: "The evangelization of the world in this generation."

Will you dream the dreams of God for your generation? Will you pray history-making prayers that will open the door for the presence of God to touch your campus or your community? Are you willing to give your life away, that a generation might live and experience true revival?

Prayer:

Holy Spirit, make Your presence known in this generation! We are desperate for You to pour out with power from on high—that ALL would be drawn to seek You and to love You—seeing Your beauty and Your worth! Let us be a generation that seeks Your face, with clean hands and a pure heart—who will open up the gates for the King of Glory in our college campuses, churches, and communities!

Take my life and use it for Your glory! Consume me with longing for Your presence at all times. Give me a holy hunger and desperation for You, that cannot be satisfied until You come in all of

Your fullness—until the dreams of Your heart are fulfilled in this generation and on the earth!

Chis Ngai is a campus minister at Arizona State and member of Collegiate Day of Prayer Leadership Team.

Evangelistic Boldness

BY SKYLER FARLEY

"But to stop this thing from spreading any
further among the people, we must warn
them to speak no longer in this name."

Acts 4:17

In Acts 4, the Sanhedrin became convinced that if the disciples continued speaking publicly in Jesus' Name, the Jesus movement was going to spread. Have you come to the same conclusion? Do you believe that if Christians boldly share Christ, empowered by the Holy Spirit, the Gospel will inevitably sweep through campuses and cities like wildfire?

A Barna research poll once showed that only 53% of millennials confidently believe that evangelism with the goal of converting another to Christianity is appropriate. This means almost half a generation of Christians on earth today believe it is inappropriate to evangelize!

Thankfully, among Gen Z the statistics are more encouraging. Barna says that, "Gen Z rarely associates negative emotions with faith sharing." However, 53% of Gen Z believe in "letting your actions speak, rather than using words to explain your faith to someone." It has been rightly said, "'Preach the Gospel always and use words if necessary' is like saying, 'Feed the starving and use food when necessary.'" The Gospel must not only be demonstrated, it must also be articulated. We must consider where these contemporary attitudes toward evangelism are coming from when the biblical witness and the role of the Holy Spirit so clearly underscore the importance and necessity of evangelism.

Jesus told his disciples in Acts 1:8, "you will receive power when the Holy Spirit comes on you; and you will be my witnesses. . . ." The Holy Spirit has not been poured out for goosebumps, but for Gospel proclamation. The Holy Spirit has come to turn men and women into witnesses for Christ and that is exactly what we see in the lives of the earliest Jesus followers. Everywhere we find disciples, they are bearing witness to Christ. Standing in front of a beggar without two coins to rub together, they witness. Brought before the Sanhedrin, they witness. Brought before angry mobs, they witness. Scattered by persecution, they witness. Brought before governors, prefects, and proconsuls, they witness. Brought before jailers, they witness. Led to the gallows, they witness. In the marketplace, in the academic halls, in the synagogues, and from home to home, they witness. Everywhere you find disciples, they are speaking without reservation in the name of Jesus. As a result, the Jesus movement could not be contained.

Acts 4:13 records, "When they saw the courage of Peter and John and realized that they were unschooled, ordinary men, they were astonished and they took note that these men had been with Jesus." The word used for "courage" or "boldness" in the original language specifically points to "freedom in speaking and unreservedness in speech." It was precisely this boldness—speaking publicly in Jesus' Name—the Sanhedrin was anxious to shut down. However, the earliest Jesus followers refused to be silenced. They not only saw themselves as fulfilling a specific command by preaching the Gospel (Jesus in words), they also were inwardly compelled to do so. In their own words, "we cannot help speaking about what we have seen and heard" (Acts 4:20).

We must regain the same heart-level conviction about speaking in Jesus' Name. May we say as Paul said in 1 Corinthians 9:16, "I am compelled to preach. Woe to me if I do not preach the gospel!" The enemy will continue to threaten and intimidate relentlessly in an attempt to get us to stop speaking, but at the end of the day we've seen too much and we've heard too much to stay quiet. The effect Christ has had on our lives compels us to speak. We must tell people about Jesus!

I believe that the antichrist spirit was animating the Sanhedrin as they tried to shut down the spread of the Jesus movement. I believe today it is no different. The antichrist spirit is still threatening and intimidating believers to prevent them from speaking boldly in Jesus' Name. Notice how you are under little threat today if you speak of spirituality or "god" in vague, ambiguous terms. However, if you speak unambiguously in the name of Jesus, the same antichrist spirit rears its head in an attempt to silence you. Praise God we are not under that spirit! We are those who confess Christ as Lord. We have been given God's very own Spirit and the Holy Spirit loves to testify to the power in Jesus' Name. "Salvation is found in no one else, for there is no other name under heaven given to mankind by which we must be saved" (Acts 4:12). Let us take up that Name and that message with fresh boldness in our generation.

Often boldness isn't activated in our lives until we act. There is a resident anointing inside every follower of Jesus to bear witness to Christ. When we begin to open our mouths and tell others about Jesus we will find the Holy Spirit rising up inside of us to bear witness. It's as if as we are saying, "Jesus heals," "Jesus saves," "Jesus loves you," "Jesus died on the cross for your sins," "Jesus has risen from the dead," the Holy Spirit stands up within us and bears witness saying, "Yes!," "this is true!," "absolutely!," "I am with you!," "I endorse this message!"

Without fail I have watched transformation take place in individuals as they step out to evangelize. Those who begin with butterflies in their stomach often report feeling "fully alive" after they have shared Christ with someone.

Are you ready to take that step and become a bold witness for Christ?

Prayer:

Father, I ask that You would make me a bold witness for Christ. I ask that the name of Jesus would spread rapidly throughout college campuses and universities across the globe. Use me in that move of Your Spirit! In Jesus' Name, Amen.

Skyler Farley is an evangelist and vice president of campus movement & training for Ignite Movement.

DAY 10

Christ-Centered Unity among Believers

BY CLINTON SCOGGINS

"May they become perfectly one, so that the world may know that You sent Me and loved them even as You loved Me."
John 17:23

Music is such a universal phenomenon, spanning different languages, cultures, regions, styles, and time periods. If one were to sing or play a note at a particular frequency, it could produce a recognizable sound. When you string notes together, you get melodies. When you add frequencies together on top of one another you can get beautiful harmonies, and striking dissonances. Volume, timbre, repetition, and so much more all shape what is produced when brought together. Consider some of your favorite music and the different elements . . . the beats, production, rhythm, voices, instruments that go into the finished product.

Much like how music comes forth from writers, composers and producers, our Father is a wonderful Creator and He designed the body of Christ with intentionality. No one part is exactly like the other. Our Father, who created humanity in His image and His likeness (Genesis 1:26-27), makes us anew in Christ Jesus as His workmanship, His masterpieces created for good works (Ephesians 2:10). Handcrafted, He knew each of us while we were yet formed in our mother's womb.

Jesus had just spent His earthly ministry demonstrating a new reality of the Kingdom of God wherever He went. He took disciples with various personalities and temperaments, and He revealed Himself to them as the Way, the Truth, and the Life. As He prepared to go to the Cross and accomplish redemption, knowing He would soon be leaving the earth, He came to Father with a number of things on His heart.

Here in John 17, in what's often called Jesus' high priestly prayer, He asks the Father for this group of disciples and those who would come after them (that's us!) that we could be caught up in the reality, the dance that the Father, Son and Spirit have eternally co-existed in. Our God who is One, yet three Persons of love, invites us to become children of God, co-heirs with Christ, the temple of the Holy Spirit and so much more, not just as individuals but as a multi-faceted dwelling place of God. He takes uniquely designed individuals and creates a holy family who will reveal Him to the world.

As Jesus asked the Father that we would be one, He declares that it is so that the world may know who Jesus is. Jesus desired that through our oneness, the world would know this same perfect love that compelled Jesus to die for us while we were yet sinners, the same love that the Father, Son and Spirit have participated in for eternity. There is a catalytic witness in the oneness of the body of Christ.

With each instrument, pitch, voice, rhyme scheme, beat, syncopation, improvisation, rest, harmony, all aligned with our Head, there is a sound and aroma produced pleasing to our Father and that shines a light to the world around us. It's heavenly, other-worldly.

What does this mean for your campus or area? Paul would often write to the people of God in particular cities and regions where the gospel had been planted.

Imagine the campus, or place that you dwell in like this. Take a moment to ask the Father for how He views you, your campus, your city or region and the Body of Christ who dwell there.

Ask the Father for His eyes to see, and His heart for the Body of Christ in your area. How could you reach out to other parts of the Body of Christ to build relationships with them? Are there roots that have created walls and divisions? Ask the Father for His divine strategy for healing and the flourishing of the Body of Christ to function as He desires it, so that the world may know Jesus.

Prayer:

Heavenly Father, give me Your heart for the oneness of Your people. By Your Spirit, bring forth Christ-centered united movements across campuses in America and the nations of the earth, so that the world may know Jesus. May "all the ends of the earth remember and turn to you LORD, and all the families of the nations worship before You" (Psalm 22:27).

Clinton Scoggins is national team member of Ignite Movement and Civil Righteousness.

Engaging Unreached Campuses

BY JOE CHAU

"And Jesus said to him, 'Today salvation
has come to this house, since he also is
a son of Abraham. For the Son of Man
came to seek and to save the lost.'"
Luke 19:9-10

L ate one night, in the basement of Baker Dorm at the University
of Massachusetts, I met with a young freshman named Mike,
who identified as gay and came from a Catholic background.

Mike had been coming to our freshmen Bible study on campus
and simultaneously volunteering at the Stonewall Center, one of the
first LGBTQ advocacy centers established on a college campus in
the US.

On this particular night, Mike's guards were down. After weeks
of creating safe spaces where Mike felt loved and cared for, he finally
began opening up in a way that was transparent, unfiltered and raw.

He shared about everything from family drug addiction, to homo-erotica, to Catholicism, to abandonment. Everything was coming out as his walls were coming down. Brick by brick, it was all coming down. "You know God doesn't see you as an abomination. Your Heavenly Father loves you. . . .", I replied, "So much so, that He gave His only son for you. . . . "

Of course it stands to reason that if you reach the campus today, you reach the world tomorrow. After all, the college students of today are the leaders of tomorrow. And likewise, if the Lifeway studies are true and 7 out of 10 high school students coming from a Bible-believing Christian church will stop practicing their faith after 2 years at a secular school, then we must not cede this high ground to the enemy and let so many become just another spiritual casualty. And if 90% of people who make a decision to follow Jesus truly do so before the age of 20, how can you not look upon the campus with the most severe urgency? Decisions and habits formed in college will likely carry for a lifetime. College students transitioning to a new environment are more open to new ideas and relations than ever before. And after their time in this cradle of spiritual, ideological, intellectual and emotional formation we call the college campus, their course seems all but set. Indeed, one can scarcely think of a more crucial mission field than the college campus.

And yet the truth is that over 50% of the college campuses in the United States have no known gospel community. Let that sink in. Over half of the campuses in America have no known community of believing students or faculty with the expressed intent (mission) to share the Good News of Jesus Christ with the students of their campus. No fellowship of students inviting other students into a life-changing relationship with Jesus. A relationship which is the source of experiencing the joy and freedom that our Heavenly Father so generously gives. The heart of our Savior is that all will come to know Him and all would be lavished with His love.

In the gospel of Luke we see Jesus breaking down all kinds of barriers to be with Zacchaeus. Yearning and longing to bring salvation; seeking out Zacchaeus with passion and purpose in order to woo Zacchaeus to Himself and call him His beloved. Jesus clear intent was "to seek and save the lost."

SINCE God passionately loves students like Mike, and as His children, should not our hearts beat as one with His? That night, Mike met a God who loved him more than he could possibly imagine. But what about the 50% of college campuses that have no known Gospel community with a clear intent to reach the lost? What about the campuses who have no one to proclaim God's love?

Prayer:

Lord, I want my heart to beat as one with Yours. Over and over again, You would go to those who seemed the furthest away from You. You went to the tax collectors. You went to the Samaritans and Gentiles. You went to the Pharisees. You went to the prostitutes, You went to the lepers. Indeed they may have been far socially, spiritually, culturally, ethically, even ethnically, but they were never far from Your heart. Forgive me for my apathy. Forgive me for my hesitation. Forgive my love of comfort. Renew a right spirit within me. And remake my heart to beat as one with Yours. Amen.

Joe Chau leads CRU Gen-Z Innovation Team and serves on the steering committee of Every Campus.

PART 3

Reaching Beyond for City Renewal

God has dreams for individual people. But He also has dreams for the Cities of the Earth. The Bible begins with a perfect man and woman in a garden and ends with a Perfect Bride and Bridegroom in a city. The Apostle John says in Revelation 21:2 "I saw the Holy City, the New Jerusalem, coming down out of heaven from God, prepared as a bride beautifully for her husband." Throughout the Bible and all of history, cities play powerful roles in God's redemptive plan.

While the New Jerusalem is a type of God's dream for every city, "harlot" Babylon is a biblical metaphor for how cities demonstrate man's pride in league with demonic principalities. It is safe to say that in this Age, every city represents both potentials. The praying church is God's agent for bringing His dream for each city into being. The Greek word used for church in the New Testament, *ekklesia,* means governing body. Though typically a politically weak minority, God's people are His Plan A for redeeming the world. In His Sermon on the Mount, Jesus describes His disciples as salt, pushing back against spiritual decay, and light, demonstrating with bright righteousness the values of an Age to Come.

One has only to read how God sent His reluctant prophet, Jonah, to Nineveh, to see that God cares about the condition of our cities. When Jonah complains that God was willing to show compassion to a sworn enemy of Israel, God replies in Jonah 4:11, "But Nineveh has more than one hundred and twenty thousand people who cannot tell their right hand from their left, and many cattle as well. Should I not be concerned about that great city?"

Oh that God would cause us to be that concerned about our cities! He has placed His governing authority on Gospel communities through unified prayer and action with Jesus—who is reigning on Heaven's Throne. Through what seems like simple unified prayer and action we bring His Kingdom to earth. As our love for Jesus and faithful living increases within the context of community and action, His Light will break forth and increase in our cities!

Lest we think that our prayers do not matter, or that we are too small in number to affect change, the story of Abraham's prayers for Sodom and Gomorrah is sobering. In Genesis 18:16-33, three visitors representing God Himself come to Abraham's tent. God invites Abraham to pray for how God will decide to deal with the spiritual crisis of those cities. Abraham had family there. He had a heart to see those cities spared from judgment for their wickedness. God is inviting us today to contend for the righteousness of His Kingdom in the cities where we live and other cities in need of His mercies.

Use these devotions to say "yes" in your own heart to God's invitation to pray for the city where you live. Our prayers of faith, in line with His merciful heart, can change the destinies of whole cities! And our redemptive actions can give Jesus more to work with when He brings His Kingdom fully to the Earth!

Healthy City-Reaching Churches

BY JOSEPH MATTERA

"They devoted themselves to the apostles'
teaching and to fellowship, to the
breaking of bread and to prayer."

Acts 2:42

Jesus said that the gates of hell will not prevail against the Church (Matthew 16:18). This illustrates the importance Jesus placed upon the local church as His Body. Truly the Church is the visible manifestation of the invisible Christ (Ephesians 1:22-23).

That being said, the significance of the Church as the Body of Christ cannot be over-emphasized!

The reason why Jesus advanced the Church as victorious over and against demonic forces of hell was because of her missional calling to spread the gospel by planting churches and making disciples who will change the world (Acts 1:8-9).

Jesus did not mention any other entity or organization with the capacity and calling to overcome the gates of hell. For example, He did not say we will overcome the evil one by political parties, economics, businesses, or military might. Only the Church can overcome the negative influence of the evil one over the world.

Even unbelieving citizens who opposed Christianity felt threatened by the power the Church had to turn the world order upside down (Acts 17:6). However, in order for the Church to function as the salt of the earth and light of the world, (Matthew 5:13-16), there are certain principles she has to follow to be effective.

The key passage to reflect on regarding these principles is Acts 2:42 which says, "they continued steadfastly in the apostles' doctrine and fellowship in the breaking of bread and in prayers" (NKJV).

This passage was given after about three thousand Jews responded to Peter's message on the Day of Pentecost (Acts 2:41).

It is interesting that the word disciple is not used again until Acts 6:7. Why? Because the newly added members of the church had to go through this Acts 2:42 process of maturation before they were considered true disciples.

They continued steadfastly in the apostles doctrine. This word "doctrine" comes from the Greek word *Didache* which means "the teaching." Hence, there was a systematic approach to learning both the Gospel and how to apply it in the context of the Church and in their everyday lives. Paul called this a "pattern of sound teaching" (2 Timothy 1:13) Pattern here means a sketch or pattern to imitate. I.E.—When a new person was added to the Church, he or she immediately was baptized (initiated into the Church) and began to learn the "first principles of the faith" so he or she would have a proper foundation and understanding of the Gospel of Jesus. (Matthew 28:19,20; Hebrews 5:12-6:4).

The early Church was focused primarily on making disciples, not merely garnering huge crowds.

They continued steadfastly in the fellowship. Christianity in the first century was primarily a way of life, not an institution. The word fellowship here (*koinonia*) means a partnership, communion, or common union with one another. Hence, the Church did not merely come together for a weekly church service; they did life together.

They continued steadfastly in the breaking of bread. The Church functioned as a family of families and shared a common meal—house to house and in the temple. The common meal culminated with the celebration of the Lord's Supper which was another way they were able to proclaim the death, burial and resurrection of Christ (1 Corinthians 11:26).

They continued steadfastly in prayers. The book of Acts can be called "The book of prayer" since it showed how prayer was involved in almost every major event of Gospel proliferation (starting with the initial 10-day prayer meeting before Pentecostal power broke forth (Acts 1, 2). The early Church knew that mere doctrine, fellowship and sacramentalism wasn't enough if they were not a people of prayer and intercession.

Church history also tells us that it was the habit of the early Church to fast and pray at least two times per week, and that they had corporate prayer three times per day (see Acts 3:1).

In conclusion, the key to gospel advancement is to have healthy city reaching churches that follow the pattern of Acts 2:42.

Prayer:

God, Your design for the Church is so powerful. I desire that and nothing less. Restore the priority of corporate spiritual formation within Your Church. Help me to practice Your way, not alone, but with others in community. Through our daily disciplines of prayer, fasting, fellowship, and breaking of bread would You multiply

Your work and cause healthy churches to come forth. Let our cities be reached with the visible fruit of the Gospel that comes from a healthy Church.

Joseph Mattera is an internationally known author, consultant, theologian, and founding pastor of Resurrection Church.

Evangelism with Community

BY DANIEL MIRONICHENKO

"After they prayed, the place where they were meeting was shaken. And they were all filled with the Holy Spirit and spoke the word of God boldly.
Acts 4:31

Our early Church fathers were living the example that Jesus modeled for them as they walked with Him: prayer and proclamation. These two realities were inseparable for the disciples. They had witnessed the priority that Jesus had for prayer and how it fueled His public ministry. As the disciples now returned to the furnace of prayer, they experienced another outpouring that would empower their bold witness in the city.

It is the Spirit that manifests Jesus through us as we preach the Gospel. It is Him burning in us with the message of the Gospel that compels the lost to come to Jesus and repent from their sins. It is the

Holy Spirit filling us continually as we live a life of prayer together in community. This is the pattern we see laced throughout the book of Acts, a consistent rhythm of prayer and proclamation in the lives of the early Church.

Notice that the apostles had just returned from being arrested by authorities and severely threatened to not speak in the name of Jesus (Acts 4:1-22). Persecution was inspiring their prayers, as well as the words of Jesus who said "blessed are you when people insult you, persecute you and falsely say all kinds of evil against you because of me" (Matthew 5:11). It is the Presence and power of the Spirit that quickens us to not shy back in fear or intimidation, but to continue to go and preach the Gospel of Jesus!

Four times in this passage above "they" is mentioned, expressing the corporate unity that they possessed with their "companions." "They prayed," "they assembled," "they were filled," and "they spoke the word of God boldly." Their unified lifestyle had brought them together for a compelling and powerful demonstration of the Gospel in their city. The unified witness of the early Church must compel us to live pursuing a similar pattern in our community living. Such a demonstration is powerful as we say "yes" together to this call of prayer and proclamation.

When I was in my early twenties, I committed Friday evenings to go and preach the Gospel on the downtown streets of my city. Every Friday, as floods of people came out to drink and party, we would preach repentance and the Love of Christ pleading with the lost to come to Christ. To this day, every Friday, my community and I go and exalt the name of Jesus in our city. From open air preaching, to one-on-ones, to tracts, to worship, we do it all because Jesus is worthy!

As we put feet on the ground for His Name's sake, we see the power of the Gospel go forth and that changes lives forever.

Today, I call you and your community into the beautiful call to go and preach Christ! To give the public witness of the gospel to the lost. God will bear witness by the Spirit to the preaching of His word, He always does! So be sent in His love and power!

Prayer:

God, may Your Spirit burn in me to love the lost and be a bold witness to those in my city. Lord, show me where I can be faithful to go and publicly proclaim the Gospel in my region and see Your Kingdom come, Amen.

Daniel Mironichenko is the founder and director of SOLD Schools.

Biblical Justice

BY JARED FONCECA

"You are the light of the world. A city set on a hill cannot be hid. . . . Let your light so shine before men, that they may see your good works and give glory to your Father who is in heaven."
Matthew 5:14-16

There is currently a stirring in the earth surrounding the issue of justice, and it's not limited to the Body of Christ. Unfortunately, the secular realm has taken charge in addressing the issues of justice when the premier agent of justice should be the Body of Christ. Why? Because at the core of the Gospel lies the issue of justice. The very foundation of the throne of God is righteousness and justice. The establishment of justice is central to both the first and second coming of Jesus. The cross is about justice. Jesus cares about justice, because He is the Just One.

Before we dive into the call to biblical justice for our cities, let's quickly build a framework. Theology should inform our thinking and ideas. We need right theology (orthodoxy) that gives birth to right action (orthopraxy). Dr. John Frame has attempted to provide us with a working definition of theology that marries these two concepts together in saying that theology is "the application of God's Word by persons in every area of life." Even though we have the Word of God, it needs to be correctly understood and applied to fully benefit from its wisdom. The Gospel is sufficient to answer our cities' cry for justice. But much of what we consider justice is mostly humanism because it is not grounded in the biblical perspective of justice.

Biblical justice must begin with our need to be justified in the courts of heaven through the blood and sacrifice of Jesus. As we receive the gift of salvation, we are birthed into the family of God and experience continual, personal transformation through the power of the Holy Spirit. We must also embrace the reality of what it means to be citizens of the Kingdom of God. The Kingdom comes with a new ethos and culture, which we must embody as the Church. Jesus has commissioned us to initiate true justice movements in our cities that will be prophetic pictures and downpayments of the justice that will be released at His second coming. Praise be to God!

The implications of biblical justice are vast. They not only deal with our personal need for justification but also the social issues that plague our cities. The Gospel addresses the issues of poverty, misogyny, law enforcement, abortion, trafficking, economic oppression, racism, education, medicine, public service, immigration laws, refugees, fatherlessness, etc. We must not choose between only addressing things as "spiritual" or "natural," because there is tremendous overlap. They both must be addressed. There is not a single issue in our cities that God cannot invade and transform through His power.

We live in a society seeking to inundate us with an extreme value for individualism, which seeks to silence the corporate cry for justice. This must not be! The Church is a new society that is qualitatively different from the culture surrounding us. Such a new society is relevant to broken cities, because it springs forth from God's own restorative justice plan.

The saints who make up this new society live their faith in the face of the same day-to-day problems as the world around them. They face the same issues as unbelievers, yet find joy in suffering, and administer mercy and justice rather than judgment and oppression, live at peace instead of hatred, raise responsible and compassionate children as a contribution to society, and serve as fathers and mothers to the orphans. Christian faith, and thus biblical justice, becomes relevant and paramount for the rebuilding of our cities. Imagine a group of people joined in the common task of seeing God's Kingdom becoming incarnate in their lives, their work, their families, their communities, and ultimately in their cities. This is biblical justice unto city renewal. This will be relevant to our cities because it lives the life of the Kingdom *in* the world, not apart from it.

We make the Gospel visible and tangible. This is not optional. We are God's primary vehicle for bringing justice and restoration to our cities and communities. As saints, we must take on our God-ordained identity as representatives of Christ's Kingdom where we live and dwell. We must ask ourselves: do we believe God has placed us in our cities to engage justice issues with Gospel solutions?

Prayer:

Father, let me and my community of faith learn to devote ourselves to good works for pressing needs, that we would not be unfruitful and that You may be glorified. Amen"

Jared Fonceca is the pastor of his family, a Fellowship of Christian Athletes staff member, and a member of Ignite Movement National Team.

Engaging the Orphan Crisis

BY JOSH KAPPES

"Imitate God, therefore, in everything you
do, because you are his dear children. Live a
life filled with love, following the example of
Christ. He loved us and offered himself as a
sacrifice for us, a pleasing aroma to God."
Ephesians 5:1-2

Paul took the first three chapters of his letter to the Church at Ephesus to lay out the incredible love of God for us displayed through His Son, Jesus Christ. He doesn't give a single command for them to do until he has made that point clear. Then he shifts in chapter 4 to basically say, now that you know, see, and understand just how deeply you are loved, live this way.

Ephesians 5:1 follows this model: Imitate God. How? As a dearly loved child. It doesn't say, if you want to be a dearly loved child, then imitate God. We are dearly loved children, adopted into God's family because we were once alienated or orphaned from His family. But now, through Christ, we are His dearly loved kids.

People who know this reality are fully equipped to live extravagant lives of love to people who desperately need the love of Christ. I can't think of a group of people who need this love more than orphans in our world today. Who is better prepared to love them than people who were once spiritual orphans until they were adopted into God's eternal family.

According to the Adoption and Foster Care Analysis and Reporting System, approximately 400,000 kids are currently in Foster Care in the United States. What organization in the world is better equipped to engage with this crisis than the church? Psalm 68:5-6 says, "A father to the fatherless, a defender of widows, is God in his holy dwelling. God sets the lonely in families."

Notice it doesn't say He places the lonely in orphanages and group homes. He places them in families.

You may be wondering how you can practically engage with the orphan crisis. Here are a few practical ways to engage and make a difference:

1. Foster a child in foster care. You might be thinking "uh. . . . I'm too young for that or I'm not married yet." My good friend Carina at the age of 19 started the foster care journey so that when she turned 21 could begin fostering a child. She's been a foster mom for a medically fragile child for almost 2 years now and she is my hero.
2. Offer meals and child care to families in your church who are fostering/adopting.
3. Find a local DSS or agency and find out what needs exist and mobilize your network to jump in and serve.
4. Live out and talk about a biblical ethic of family and sexuality.

Go back to our feature verse. Live a life of love modeled after Jesus, who offered Himself as a sacrifice for us. Engaging in the orphan crisis will undoubtedly require sacrificial love, but remember, the same Jesus who gave himself for us, lives in us. He will empower us to live out a life of sacrificial love to our orphan neighbors.

Prayer:

God, I was once an orphan, stranded from my Home—You. Thank You for making a way through Jesus for me to be brought back into Your loving arms. Thank You for Your sacrificial love. You are a good, loving, and active Father. Give me a heart for those who are not only spiritually stranded but also physically homeless. Give me a heart for orphans. Show me how You desire to use me to bring the lonely into my family. Give me the courage and means to move forward in living this out sacrificially.

Josh Kappes is the vice president of Love Life USA.

Caring for the Marginalized

BY MICHELLE GILL

> "'This is the most important [commandment],'
> answered Jesus, 'Hear O Israel, the Lord
> our God, the Lord is One. Love the Lord
> your God with all your heart and with
> all your soul and with all your mind and
> with all your strength.' The second is this:
> 'Love your neighbor as yourself.' No other
> commandment is greater than these."
> **Mark 12:29-31**

Throughout high school and college I would often pray and ask God to reveal my calling to me. One day it finally clicked for me and I saw that the simplest and purest commandment was right in front of me: to love God and love my neighbor as myself. I didn't have to move countries or cities to find my calling. Jesus was calling me to STAY. To stay and love my neighbor. I found peace in the simplicity of the calling. All that I needed to do was commit to intentionally love those around me. I began to see people differently; God opened my eyes to my own neighbors who had experienced life differently than me, neighbors who were marginalized. Jesus called me to do life with people, to stay with people in their joy and to stay with people in their pain. Jesus called me to love people the way He loves them.

One of my neighbors who I felt called to love reached out to me after not being around for nearly a year. She is in an unhealthy relationship that consumes her time and prevents her from coming around. However, when they break-up, she reaches back out and wants to hang out and pretend that everything in her life is good. This has happened multiple times over the past three years.

At first, I was super frustrated because it felt like a rejection of the friendship I had worked to develop with her. The fact that she would leave and not respond to me for months and only reach out when she needed something left me confused and hurt.

When I prayed about the situation, I felt Jesus gently remind me of His grace. *Michelle, how are you going to be frustrated with her? Isn't that what you do to me? When you leave me and think you know better, am I not always here when you come back? I never expect you to have it all together. Do I not gently take your hand and work through one thing at a time with you? If I expected you to be perfect, you would never want to reach out to me either. It is not about you. I have called you to represent Jesus to her. Is my grace not sufficient enough for YOU?*

So when she reached out the next time time, I relied on the grace that Jesus so freely gave me. I gently took time to spend with her and to love her even though I knew she wasn't going to stay. I knew she would go back to the unhealthy relationship. But I also knew that I was building trust, a safe place for her to come and receive hope.

I don't have a conclusion for her story, but I return to the calling of Jesus over my life: the invitation to STAY and continue to put into action the Greatest Commandment. I continue to yield my heart to the guidance of the Holy Spirit.

If you are trying to figure out your calling, I would encourage you to simply obey the Greatest Commandment, love the Lord your God with all your heart and love your neighbor as yourself. God will use you regardless of your age to love and care for the people to whom He calls you. All you need to do is give Him your yes.

What neighbor is Jesus calling you to love?

Prayer:

Jesus I repent for the times in my life when I have rejected You. Please remove any self-righteousness that I have in my heart. Humble me to love those who are marginalized. Empower me to see them as individuals You created and love. Give me grace to keep showing up in my neighbors' lives whom You have called me to love. Amen.

Michelle Gill is the co-founder and leader of Hope House, an inner-city ministry.

Christ-Centered Unity in a City

BY BRIAN ALARID

"Be completely humble and gentle; be patient, bearing with one another in love. Make every effort to keep the unity of the Spirit through the bond of peace. There is one body and one Spirit, just as you were called to one hope when you were called; one Lord, one faith, one baptism; one God and Father of all, who is over all and through all and in all."

Ephesians 4:2-6

Today, our nation is more polarized and divided than at any time since the 1960s. Division and animosity have seeped into the Church as well, and, by and large, we have not been credible witnesses to the people around us.

Having been a pastor for over 25 years, I have found that the best way to confront this divisiveness is united prayer. I believe it's going to take the whole Church, united in prayer, to present the Gospel to a broken and hurting world. Only a united Church can heal a divided city and a divided nation. Nothing has the power to unite a fragmented Church like Christ-centered prayer.

For 22 years, I lived in Albuquerque, New Mexico, and together with many other pastors and leaders from diverse backgrounds, we saw God unite our city through prayer. The fruit of that prayer-fueled unity was measurable and documented societal transformation. We learned that in order to build and sustain Christ-centered unity in a city, we must make three commitments:

1. A Commitment to the Supremacy of Christ

We must make a radical commitment to the supremacy of Christ as seen in Colossians 1:18: "And [Christ] is the head of the body, the church; he is the beginning and the firstborn from among the dead, so that in everything he might have the supremacy." When Jesus is the central focus of city-wide prayer efforts, and not merely a gratuitous add-on, unity begins to gain real traction. However, if the basis of our unity is theology, ecclesiology, worship style, political persuasion, or anything else other than Christ and Him crucified, even our most noble efforts are bound to fail.

2. A Commitment to Humility

Without a commitment to humility, pride will destroy every unity movement. That's why Paul challenged us to be *completely* humble before he talks about unity in Ephesians 4:2-3: "Be completely humble and gentle; be patient, bearing with one another in love. Make every effort to keep the unity of the Spirit through the bond of peace." Paul understood from his relationship with Barnabas how difficult it is to maintain unity. Unity will only exist where there is genuine humility.

The biggest obstacle to unity is pride and the greatest catalyst for unity is humility. Unity takes more than effort. We have to lay down our pride and clothe ourselves with the humility of Christ. And by laying down our pride, I mean our personal pride, our ministry pride, our theological pride, and our denominational pride. We must learn to prefer others above ourselves and love them with Christ's love. To obtain the favor and blessing of God promised in Psalm 133, we have to stop building our own "kingdoms" and instead focus on unity with other believers and churches.

3. A Commitment to United Prayer

Dr. A.T. Pierson made this profound statement, "There has never been a spiritual awakening in any country or locality that did not begin in united prayer." Prayer is the language that moves heaven and unites God's people on Earth.

George Otis Jr. observed, "United prayer is a declaration to the heavenlies that a community of believers is prepared for divine partnership. When this welcoming intercession is joined by knowledge, it becomes focused, leading to and sustaining the kind of fervent prayer that produces results."

If you want to see change in your city, join forces with other like-minded believers, and make these three commitments together: "We will keep Christ Supreme, we will prefer one another in humility, and we will unite in prayer." Results will undoubtedly follow and your city will never be the same.

Prayer:

God, I desire and pray for unity in the Church of my city. Give us a revelation of You that would cause our hearts to become one. We declare that You will have the first place in our hearts, our relationships, our churches, and thus in our cities! We lay ourselves and our rights down. Let Your Kingdom, not our own, come, in our city. Bind us together in love through united prayer! Let us release heaven on earth and see Your hand moving, throughout our city, because we have chosen to center our unity on Christ! In Jesus Name! Amen!

Brian Alarid is the president of America Prays and World Prays and the Chairman of Pray for All.

PART 4

Reaching Beyond to the Ends of the Earth

Imagine being 75 years old and receiving a call to leave "your country, your people and your father's household" for an undisclosed land the Lord will reveal to you. On the heels of this calling, God gives a grand promise, "all peoples on earth will be blessed through you," (Genesis 12:3). "So Abram went, as the Lord had told him," (Genesis 12:4).

One Bible commentator noted that this call "indicated a missionary vision that God intended Abraham's descendants to have. They were to look beyond themselves to all nations, to all the families of the earth." Charles Spurgeon similarly noted this call contained "the missionary character of the seed of Abraham."

God's plan in plucking a man from the nations to become His own special possession was always unto radiating His light to the ends of the earth. The first verse of the New Testament reads, "This is the genealogy of Jesus the Messiah the son of David, the son of Abraham," (Matthew 1:1).

God's Plan A is still intact. God is radiating the light of the Gospel revealed in the face of His Son to the ends of the earth and He is still searching for willing men and women, who will forsake the comfort of their country, people and home to spread this light.

God's heart is for all the nations of the earth. Our ears and our hearts must be tuned to the reverberating chord of the Gospel: "God so loved the world." May this same love for the people of the world be found in us. Whether we are called to serve as long-term missionaries, go on short-term missions projects, sow financially, or intercede for nations and people groups, God's heart for the nations must find expression in His children.

Jesus gave a tremendous promise in Matthew 24:14 that the Gospel would be preached to all people groups before the end comes. Because of the courage and sacrifice of generations before us, we can honestly say that we may be living in the hour of history when this promise reaches its fulfillment. The question is whether we will pick up the baton and engage with the missionary heart of Jesus in this generation.

We hope that these devotionals will inspire and challenge you to look beyond yourself, beyond your city, and even beyond your own country to consider God's heart for the nations. We believe that as you pray for and consider the persecuted Church, unreached people groups, and the salvation of Israel you will find yourself being invited to participate in God's eternal storyline.

The Salvation of Israel

BY SCOTT VOLK

"Brothers and sisters, my heart's desire
and prayer to God for the Israelites
is that they may be saved."
Romans 10:1

"All Israel will be saved."
Romans 1:26

Once sin and death were introduced into the world through Adam and Eve, the Lord put a plan into place that would ultimately offer salvation to the entire world. God was looking for a people through whom the Messiah would come, ultimately crushing the head of the devil and offering eternal life and salvation to all the nations of the earth.

The Lord chose Abraham, and ultimately the people of Israel, promising Abraham that through him, all the nations of the earth will be blessed. Miraculously, 99 year-old Abraham, whose body was 'as good as dead' along with his 89 year-old barren wife, whose womb was also dead, supernaturally conceived Isaac. And, just as the Lord promised, Abraham and his offspring found their way into the genealogy of Jesus, the Messiah of Israel and the Savior of the world.

God's Heart for Israel

There is an undeniable truth, woven throughout scripture, that we must all recognize and that truth is this: the children of Israel have been, and forever will be, dear to the heart of the Lord.

> "Who is like Your people Israel, the one nation on earth whom the Lord has redeemed to make a name for himself." (2 Samuel 7:23)

> "'Though the mountains be shaken and hills be removed, yet my unfailing love for you [Israel] will not be shaken nor my covenant of peace be removed,' says the LORD." (Isaiah 54:10)

Throughout scripture, God refers to Israel as "My people" and He does that for a specific reason. Israel is the one nation that the Lord chose that would bring salvation to all the nations of the earth.

Jesus' Heart for the Salvation of Israel

Once we see and recognize the Lord's heart for Israel, it's no surprise that Jesus carried that same heart for that people. Not only was Jesus emotionally broken and weeping over Jerusalem because they didn't receive Him, but He said some remarkable things regarding the people of Israel.

> ". . . for salvation is from the Jews." (John 4:22)

> "I was sent only to the lost sheep of Israel." (Matthew 15:24)

Paul's Heart for the Salvation of Israel

Although Paul exhorted us to rejoice in the Lord always, the issue of Israel's salvation was always something that caused him great sorrow and unceasing grief. After boldly proclaiming that there is nothing that could separate us from the love of God, he goes on to say that he wished he were cursed and separated from God, if it could mean that Israel would be saved.

God's heart is for the salvation of Israel; Jesus' heart is for the salvation of Israel; Paul's heart is for the salvation of Israel; and our hearts need to long for the salvation of Israel.

What Can We Do?

When we realize that the salvation of Israel is an ultimate issue, it's incumbent on us, as the Church, to carry this burden. Scripture says that, "salvation has come to the Gentiles to make Israel envious" (Romans 15:11). We are now carriers of the very salvation that came through Israel and the Jewish people and we're the ones called to bring them this good news of salvation.

Unfortunately, as you're reading this devotional today, the vast majority of Israel and the Jewish people are lost. Jesus said He would not return until Israel welcomed Him back. It's time for us to carry the burden of the Lord for Israel's salvation. Will you answer the call?

Prayer:

Father, I ask you to remove the blinders off the eyes of the Jewish people and reveal Your Messiah to them. May the One who they've rejected for millennia, be the One they will soon bow their knees to in salvation. According to Your Word, I pray for the peace of Jerusalem and believe You to watch over that city and protect. May Your Name be glorified among Your people Israel in Jesus' Name.

Scott Volk is the founder and director of Together for Israel.

The Fullness of the Gentiles

BY ALLEN HOOD

"For I do not desire, brethren, that you should
be ignorant of this mystery, lest you should
be wise in your own opinion, that blindness
in part has happened to Israel until the
fullness of the Gentiles has come in. And
so all Israel will be saved, as it is written:
"The Deliverer will come out of Zion, And He
will turn away ungodliness from Jacob."
Romans 11:25–26 NKJV

In this passage, Paul writes to the church in Rome, the power base of
the Gentile nations, and declares a glorious mystery—"all Israel will
be saved" at the return of the Lord Jesus. Here, Paul envisions something unique within God's plan of redemption. For the first time in
history an entire nation will be saved, and when this happens for Israel,
it will be like life from the dead for the entire world (Romans 11:15).

God has not cast His people away. In fact, Paul reminds the church in Rome that they have received the gospel because of a Jewish remnant (of which Paul is one) who have believed in Jesus Christ and taken His message to the nations (Romans 11:5).

Paul earlier shares his apostolic passion for Israel's salvation. He is willing to exchange his eternal security for his countrymen's salvation (Romans 9:1-2). He appeals to the believing Gentiles to remember with gratitude what Israel has endured to bring the earth God's glory, the covenants, the law, the service of God, the promises, the fathers of the faith, and, yes, even Christ Himself (Romans 9:3-5).

Then Paul plants a most beautiful prayer right in the heart of the world's most dominant empire: "Brethren, my heart's desire, and prayer to God for Israel is that they may be saved," (Rom. 10:1). Today, the Holy Spirit is breathing upon Paul's apostolic passion and prayer, calling a predominantly Gentile Church to touch Paul's passion and lift up Paul's prayer. Yet, there is even more. God has a wondrous plan to bring Jews and Gentiles into the next age as one new man filled with gratitude and love by linking their destinies together.

Israel's salvation and fullness as a nation will depend upon Gentile believers coming into their fullness. The fullness in Romans 11:25 is more than a quantitative reality. It is a qualitative reality, describing the quality of the Gentile's love for and obedience to Jesus Christ that leads to a great provocation of Israel to receive their Messiah. Believing Gentiles must not be ignorant of this coming great salvation at the return of the Lord, for they play a crucial part in God's plan.

The Gentile mission depended upon a Jewish remnant taking the gospel to the nations. "But you will receive power when the Holy Spirit comes on you; and you will be my witnesses in Jerusalem, and in all Judea and Samaria, and to the end of the earth" (Acts 1:8).

The salvation of Israel as an entire nation will depend upon the fullness of the Gentile believers in those nations provoking Israel to jealousy. Israel will deeply desire what Gentile believers have spiritually. In the past, Israel has not been provoked by the Church but repulsed by the well-documented antisemitism and atrocities committed against them. Yet Paul, as an apostle to the Gentiles, magnified his ministry to provoke Israel to jealousy (Romans 11:13-14). He deeply desired an offering from the nations worthy of Lord Jesus and that would provoke Israel.

"I say then, have they stumbled that they should fall? Certainly not! But through their [Israel's] fall, to provoke them to jealousy, salvation has come to the Gentiles." (Romans 11:11)

"For I speak to you Gentiles; inasmuch as I am an apostle to the Gentiles, I magnify my ministry, if by any means I may provoke to jealousy those who are my flesh and save some of them." (Romans 11:13–14 NKJV)

This is a wonderful time to be alive when God is bringing together a remnant saved by the blood of Jesus from every nation who are touching Paul's passion and crying out together with one voice for God to bring forth fullness—the fullness of the Holy Spirit in the Church, the fullness of God's glory among the nations, and the fullness of Israel at the return of Jesus. When this occurs, it will be like life from the dead for the entire world, and "the glory of God will cover the earth like the waters cover the sea" (Habakkuk 2:14).

Gentiles will enter the next age saying, "Thank you Israel for bearing the brunt of Satan for 2,000 years. Thank you for bringing forth the Covenants, the Scriptures, and the Messiah. Thank you for sharing the Gospel of Jesus Christ with us." And Israel will enter the next age saying to a Gentile remnant from every nation, "Thank you for holding the line on salvation by grace alone through faith alone in Christ Jesus alone. Thank you for being the faithful witness to the Messiah, Christ Jesus. Thank you for bearing us up and serving us in love during the last days." Both Jew and Gentile will enter the dawning age in gratitude and love. At the thought of this, Paul breaks into doxology: "Oh, the depth of the riches of the wisdom and knowledge of God! How unsearchable his judgments, and his paths beyond tracing" (Romans 11:33).

Prayer:

Father, forgive me for my ignorance of Your plan. Forgive me where I have not embraced Paul's apostolic passion, prayed Paul's apostolic prayer, and have not lived in the fullness of the Spirit's power to love and obey Jesus. Help us, Your Church, Father. Pour out the Holy Spirit upon us. Bring us into the fullness of love and obedience to Christ Jesus. Let this fullness be a great testimony to Israel that Your Son, Jesus, is both Israel's Messiah and Lord of all. In Jesus' Name, Amen.

Allen Hood is an International speaker and founder and director of Excellencies of Christ Ministries.

Unreached People Groups

BY JOHN KIM

"And this gospel of the kingdom will
be proclaimed throughout the whole
world as a testimony to all nations,
and then the end will come."
Matthew 24:14 ESV

The command to preach the Gospel to all the world has never been this clear in all of human history. In the past, the challenges to finishing the Great Commission could be due to the lack of technology, lack of resources, or inadequate access to information about people groups. We can no longer claim these as obstacles today. The task of reaching every ethno-linguistic group in our lifetime is within reach, but not without its challenges.

According to Joshua Project, an unengaged, unreached people group, or UUPG, is a people group with "no known active church planting underway." It is estimated that there are 3,050 UUPGs, which is about 278 million people around the world. In other words, the majority of Christian leaders around the world today would unanimously agree that these 278 million people would be the most difficult to reach with the Gospel of Jesus Christ. With this challenge before us, where do we begin?

Dick Eastman has said, "Prayer alone will remove every obstacle that stands in the way." The task of reaching every single people group, no matter their population, is a command given to us from our Lord Jesus. God is in the business of answering the prayer of Matthew 9:37-38, "Then he said to his disciples, 'The harvest is plentiful, but the workers are few. Ask the Lord of the harvest, therefore, to tend out workers into his harvest field.'"

We are commanded to *pray earnestly* for laborers to be sent. We've seen throughout whenever a group of committed Christ followers pray earnestly and continuously, that the burden of missions falls upon the Church because Jesus married prayer and missions in that way. When we pray, the Lord sends. He did it in the Upper Room in Jerusalem, He did it with the Moravians, He did it with the Student Volunteer Movement, and He's doing it now all over the world. He's doing it among the Koreans, Indonesians, Mongolians, Brazilians, Ukrainians, students, fathers, mothers, families, and even retired professionals.

More than a hundred years ago, my people group, formerly known as "the Hermit Kingdom," was an unengaged, unreached people group. It took the sacrificial obedience of nameless and faceless Christ-followers for the Gospel to advance in this seemingly insignificant nation. Robert Jermain Thomas is considered the first Protestant martyr in Korea. He died without even having the chance of sharing the Gospel with a Korean. The closest he got to preaching the Gospel was throwing his Bible onto the shores of Korea while he was being killed on a boat attempting to preach the Gospel. Today, close to 40% of South Koreans call themselves Christians.

Prayer:

Father I ask in the name of Your Precious Son, to send forth laborers into the hardest and darkest regions of the earth. Send Your Sons and Daughters to proclaim the Good News with boldness and clarity. Fill them with Your Spirit and Your love to bring all peoples to the saving knowledge of Jesus Christ so that they may have eternal life. I desire that Yeshua be magnified and glorified in every unreached people group, and I pray that in my lifetime, I would see every people group with a witness of the Gospel in Jesus' Name.

John Kim is the president of Kairos Global.

DAY 21

The Persecuted Church

BY CARL MOELLER

"But I tell you, love your enemies and pray for
those who persecute you, that you may be
children of your Father in heaven. He causes his
sun to rise on the evil and the good, and sends
rain on the righteous and the unrighteous."
Matthew 5:44–45

The Yalu and Tumen Rivers form a natural meandering boundary between The People's Republic of China and The Democratic People's Republic of North Korea. Night and day, soldiers from both armies stare vigilantly at each other through high-powered field glasses as they control traffic in and out of their respective countries. Those approaching the border checkpoints find that travel moves at a snail's pace, for each is high risk and high security. Very few people are allowed to cross the heavily fortified border regularly. Traveling inside North Korea is almost impossible.

But one man does go around the country, known only as "The Traveler." He helps distribute goods to persecuted believers inside

North Korea. Despite the ever-present danger of exposure, The Traveler remains an unpretentious and simple man. He's adept at blending in, remaining both vigilant and decisive. It's a matter of survival. He has served these brothers and sisters for years, and his real name is a mystery. That is intentional. The fewer people who know it, the better, for if his secret work on behalf of God's people were ever to be discovered, it would mean a brutal death sentence for him.

When I spoke to him, I asked him what the church in North Korea prays for. This ostensibly emotionless man who puts his life on the line every day—often for people he's never even met living in cities he's never visited—began to weep. He told me of a church movement that has remained underground ever since the 1950s. Back then, entire congregations were forced into the streets and run over with bulldozers by the evil regime. Thousands of men, women, and children were literally crushed to death, their remains compacted, recycled, and used to line roadbeds throughout the surrounding cities.

Today, direct descendants of those who were left behind form the remnant of believers. And they are a praying Church. It's simple. Believers in North Korea—and those throughout the persecuted Church—don't see prayer as an add-on activity. It's not like they have a relationship with God and prayer is just one activity in that relationship. Theirs is foundationally a praying Church, and their relationship with God is a foundationally prayer relationship. It is completely integrated in a way that ours in the West just isn't. They have a wealth of painful experiences that we have seldom tasted. When they come together for corporate prayer, it's almost sanctified desperation. Someone leads out, and then everyone in the room prays, passionately, often multiple times. They pray for things we probably wouldn't think to pray for, and never pray for many of the things we do.

Much of our prayer comes in response to a dutiful call to improve our lax spiritual disciplines. We're supposed to pray in our church services, so we do. We're supposed to pray for our food, so we do, quietly and quickly, especially if we are out in public. We rarely have to pray out of a sense of dependence, and so we often don't.

North Korean believers are prayerfully focused on one purpose: to be able to fulfill God's will for their lives. Their prayer is a prayer for liberation, for lifting of the darkness, for a possibility to reopen the churches of their ancestors, and for reconciliation; and astonishingly, they pray for the salvation of North Korea's dictator Kim Jong-Un.

So despite the dangers, The Traveler continues to equip believers with commentaries, Bibles, radio resources, training, and encouragement to keep them focused on the Lord. In a country where a church is completely underground and believers rarely meet, believers often pray alone, but they pray with one voice. The Traveler knows that if there's ever going to be freedom there, it will be because of prayer. And prayer already makes them truly free in Christ.

Prayer:

Father, remind me of the dependence on You that our persecuted brothers and sisters have. Allow me to pray for the persecuted—and for those who persecute them. Draw me into a deeper, more desperate prayer life where my only goal is bringing You Glory through fulfilling Your will in my life. Amen.

Dr. Carl Moeller is the executive director of the Joshua Fund.

DOXOLOGY

"Missions is not the ultimate goal of the church. Worship is. Missions exists because worship doesn't. Worship is ultimate, not missions, because God is ultimate, not man. When this age is over, and the countless millions of the redeemed fall on their faces before the throne of God, missions will be no more. It is a temporary necessity. But worship abides forever."—John Piper

There is a real day coming in human history when every nation, tribe, people and language will stand before the Lamb who sits on the Throne. The redeemed from every generation and every place on earth will gather around the throne and worship God together.

Can you imagine the sound of all those languages praising God simultaneously? Can you imagine the sight of every people group dressed in spotless robes? The fullness of the Gentiles will be represented and all of Israel will be saved. No tribe will be left out. No nation excluded. Every martyr and missionary who labored without seeing visible fruit during their lifetime, will see the harvest gathered from the same soil where they offered their lives as a sacrifice. On that day Jesus will have His perfect inheritance among the nations!

God made Abraham a promise that all the nations of the earth would be blessed through Him. This picture of every nation, tribe, people and language gathered around the Throne at the end of the Age is a guarantee of that promise. Jesus said that the Gospel would be preached to all people groups before the end (Matthew 24:14). Yet again, we have assurance that this promise will come to pass.

A Burst of Praise

While Paul was laboring among the Gentiles and contending for the salvation of his own people, he paused to consider the scope of God's eternal plan and the result was that he couldn't help but break into doxology,

> *"Oh, the depth of the riches of the wisdom and knowledge of God! How unsearchable his judgments, and his paths beyond tracing out! 'Who has known the mind of the Lord? Or who has been his counselor?' 'Who has ever given to God, that God should repay them?' For from him and through him and for him are all things. To him be the glory forever! Amen"* (Romans 11:33-36).

In the very next verse, Paul exhorts all of his listeners in light of this glorious Gospel to offer their bodies as a living sacrifice, for "this is your true and proper worship" (Romans 12:1). As we consider the call to go "beyond" from this compilation of devotions, we must come to see it as our only appropriate response to the God who so loved the world that He gave His only Son for us. "Beyond" is in the ultimate sense a call to worship.

We Praise God:

As we consider all the ways God wants to transform our own hearts, as well as campuses, cities, and the nations of the earth through the reality of the Gospel, we are moved to praise Him. As we stand in this moment of redemptive history, we praise God because we know He is good. We praise God because we know that He is faithful. We praise God because He is powerful enough to fulfill every one of His good promises. We praise God for inviting us into His story and allowing us to co-labor with Him. We praise God, the Lord of the Harvest. The Desire of the Nations. To Him be the glory forever and ever. Amen.

WORKS CITED

Brown, Michael. *Our Hands Are Stained with Blood: The Tragic Story of the "Church" and the Jewish People.*

Moeller, Carl A., et al. *The Privilege of Persecution: And Other Things the Global Church Knows That We Don't.* Moody Publishers, 2011.

Rogers, David Wilson. "What it means to be anchored in faith." *Carlsbad Current Argus*, 15 September 2018, https://www.currentargus.com/story/life/faith/2018/09/15/what-means-anchored-faith/129 3732002/. Accessed 22 October 2022.

Would You Like to

Love 2 Pray

Introducing a digital ministry
that will mentor you
toward a powerful, meaningful
personal prayer life!

Go to **love2pray.com** for more information.

Love 2 Pray is a ministry of the
Church Prayer Leaders Network and *Prayer Connect* magazine.

*Prayer*CONNECT

 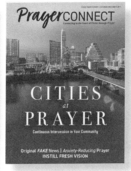 

A new quarterly magazine designed to:

Mobilize believers to pray God's purposes fortheir church, city and nation.

Connect intercessors with the growing worldwide prayermovement.

Equip prayer leaders and pastors with tools to
disciple their congregations.

Each issue of *Prayer Connect* includes:

- Practical articles to equip and inspire your prayer life.
- Helpful prayer tips and proven ideas.
- News of prayer movements around the world.
- Theme articles exploring important prayer topics.
- Connections to prayer resources available online.

Print subscription: $24.99 (includes digital version)
Digital subscription: $19.99
Church Prayer Leaders Network membership: $35.99 (includes
print, digital, and CPLN membership benefits)

SUBSCRIBE NOW.
Order at **prayerleader.com/membership**

IGNITE

M O V E M E N T

TO SEE COLLEGE CAMPUSES AND CITIES TRANSFORMED BY THE REALITY OF THE GOSPEL!

LEARN MORE ABOUT THE MOVEMENT

WWW.IGNITEMVMT.COM

Made in the USA
Coppell, TX
19 November 2019

Plants are Magic

VOLUME 4

Published by Rebecca Desnos

I'm Rebecca Desnos—a natural dyer, writer and independent publisher in the UK. I started *Plants Are Magic* magazine in 2017. It's a magazine for plant lovers about creating things with plants.

Plants Are Magic is ad-free and supported by you. Thank you for keeping the magazine alive!

Get in touch

Do you have any comments about this magazine or suggestions for future issues? I'd love to hear from you!

info@rebeccadesnos.com

Portrait by Siobhan Watts

WELCOME!

Welcome back to another issue of *Plants Are Magic* magazine! It's been a year since the last issue was released and I'm thrilled to share volume 4 with you. I hope you'll agree that it was worth the wait. As with every issue of *Plants Are Magic,* this edition has been an absolute pleasure to make.

Are there any plants that make you feel at home?

Many of my favourite plants seem to pop up just when I need them. This was my inspiration for this issue that is themed around *Home.* These plants can be a familiar comfort when we travel to new places, as Mila Wood explores on page 11: *we can take 'home' with us everywhere we go.* Alyssa Dennis explains that the remedy for what ails us is often a plant that grows right outside our door (page 25). Plants really are magic!

As a natural dyer, my favourite way of exploring plants is to sample them for their colour potential – either by testing them in my dye pot, or by simply pouring hot water over petals to see if any colour can be extracted. Incredibly, the same plants from different areas can produce different colours. Turn to page 38 to find out how to make paint from petals, and page 88 to dye with berries.

Wherever you live in the world, I hope you'll find some seeds of inspiration within the pages of *Plants Are Magic* and come across new ways to befriend your local plants. My dream is that you'll find some new ideas to delve into over the coming months!

As always, thank you for supporting this magazine!

Rebecca xx

Past editions

Catch up on volumes 1-3 by downloading the digital magazines here:

www.rebeccadesnos.com

BEETS

SPIRULINA

TURMERIC

BArley grass

CARROTS

MATCHA

102

38

Contents

Safety: *Please take care when identifying the plants highlighted in this magazine. If you have any doubt, please consult someone who is experienced or refer to an identification book. Don't eat flowers from plants that have been sprayed with chemicals. Follow the tips on page 41 to grow your own edible flowers.*

80

The plant lovers who helped make this magazine

Mila Wood is a UK-based writer and founder of plant-centred skincare and herbal remedy brand *Mila's Apothecary*. She can usually be found writing about her favourite subjects: women, mental health and plants. Otherwise, you'll likely find her in the meadows or cleaning up a kombucha explosion in the kitchen. Read Mila's piece *Belonging* on page 11. *instagram.com/milasapothecary*

Jemma Ricketts is a medical herbalist and founded *Enchanted Plants* in 2006. She creates beautiful organic skincare and soap using the finest botanicals. Read Jemma's interview on page 16 where she tells us about *Dorset Flowers* – a locally grown botanical face oil. *enchantedplants.co.uk*

Alyssa Dennis, an artist and herbalist, created her project *Common Knowledge* in 2016 as a way of connecting with her local medicinal plant allies. Alyssa believes that plants are our teachers. Her goal is to re-establish reciprocity within the ecosystems of our urban environments. Read Alyssa's article *Urban Tending* on page 25. *commonknowledgeplants.com*

Miss Wondersmith is passionate about making and sharing wonder, which can be seen through the magical events she shares with strangers and her writings about everyday wonder highlighting the natural beauty of her home, the ever-inspiring Pacific Northwest (USA). Read Miss Wondersmith's piece *Lady Fern* on page 30. *thewondersmith.com*

Bex Partridge is a nature-loving creative who predominately works with fresh and dried flowers in her practice. Bex founded *Botanical Tales* three years ago, is a trained chef and frequently uses her homegrown edible flowers in her culinary creations. Find Bex's tips for growing edible flowers on page 41. *botanicaltales.com*

Louise Gale is a British mixed media artist who creates in her studio on the sunny south coast of Spain. She loves to combine the healing power of nature with the meditative process of mandala-creating. On page 46, Louise tells us about the benefits of going barefoot and how this will boost our energy. *botanicalmandalas.com | louisegale.com*

Sophie Parker is an environmental conservationist who established *Betony & Sage* to share her passion for the natural world with others. She has worked in the conservation sector for over 10 years and continues to learn from and find solace in nature. Read Sophie's interview on page 49. *betonyandsage.co.uk*

Ocean Rose Fashakin is a multifaceted artist with roots firmly planted in botanical magic, poetry, photography, and all of the intersections they intertwine. Read Ocean's beautiful piece, *Mothering Plants,* on page 54. *instagram.com/ocean_bythesea*

Naina Bajaria specialises as an ayurvedic practitioner and yoga teacher. Through her own experiences of these sciences, she now educates and advocates yogic and ayurvedic lifestyle as means to attuning to nature's rhythms as a process of healing and spiritual growth. On page 56, Naina shows us how to rebalance our 'inner' and 'outer' homes. *nainaayurveda.com*

Jo Cauldrick is an artist from the UK who creates art decks to help others connect with the lunar cycle and bring rhythm to their lives. Jo says, *"The moon is like poetry to me, I've loved her since I was a child".* Her first book *Muse with the Moon* is out in September 2019. Jo's illustrations are on pages 63 and 65 for you to enjoy colouring in. *themoonjournal.com*

Katie-Jane Wright is a crystal whisperer and open channel for cosmic consciousness. She has been a psychic, clairvoyant and medium since her childhood. On page 66, Katie-Jane tells us how we can shower our plants with love using crystals.
andcrystals.com | katiejanewright.com

Cat is a knitter, gardener, aspiring folk herbalist and mother living in the hills of central Portugal. She has a thing for racial justice and a love affair with raw wool, and will most likely be found sipping garden tea under an olive tree, with a knitting project in hands and a podcast in ears. Read Cat's *Garden Stories* on page 75. *theolivetreesandthemoon.com*

Samorn Sanixay is a weaver, textile designer and passionate gardener. Samorn is the cofounder of *Eastern Weft*, a weaving cooperative based in Vientiane, Laos, which supports disadvantaged young Hill Tribe women through art and weaving. Read Samorn's interview on page 80.
instagram.com/samorn_sanixay | easternweft.com

Julia Watkins is a mother and a maker, who lives, creates, and writes from her home in Chicago, Illinois. She hosts the Instagram account *@simply.living.well,* where she shares about living simply, slowly and naturally as well as tips for creating less waste. Read Julia's interview on page 97.
instagram.com/simply.living.well

Jule Kebelmann is a German textile designer with a lot of love for herbs, plants and natural fibres. She brought these passions together in *Hey Mama Wolf* by producing local and sustainable knitting yarns that are naturally dyed. On page 102, Jule shares a tutorial for making lake pigments.
instagram.com/hey_mama_wolf_yarns

"I have a room all to myself; it is nature."

— Henry David Thoreau

Yarrow & ribwort plantain leaves

BELONGING

Wherever the plants are, I'm home.

Words and photos by Mila Wood

"Thousands of tired, nerve-shaken, over-civilized people are beginning to find out that going to the mountains is going home."

– John Muir, *Our National Parks.*

These words from 1901, written by naturalist and environmentalist John Muir deeply resonate with me. No matter who you are or where you have come from, why do the mountains, the meadows and the forests feel like home? For me, they instil a deep sense of peace and represent feelings of comfort, calm, familiarity, belonging and community, in much the same way as being surrounded by friends or family in a physical home with brick walls. Home is where I am free to be myself, safe from prejudice, stress

and worries, cocooned in the comfort of the familiar. Home does not have to be in a particular location or with familiar people; it can be familiar plants. Finding plant allies in all corners of the world can help us feel at home wherever we go.

One of the many ways to enhance our relationship with nature is to get to know her plants and how they can sustain and heal us. Foraging or wildcrafting – meaning to gather plants from their locations in the wild – allows for us to communicate with plants on a deeper level by utilising them for their edible and medicinal benefits. When we encounter our favourite plant friends around the world, we can perform similar foraging rituals with them. This gives us the opportunity to foster connections to new landscapes, taking "home" with us everywhere we go.

Trees

Coniferous trees have the ability to calm me just with their presence. One sunny spring day, lost somewhere in the Elbe Sandstone Mountains between Germany and the Czech Republic with an old friend, I stopped to admire how the shimmering beams of spring sunlight, full of fir pollen, danced through the conifer branches. My eyes moved to the ends of the branches that were covered in fresh young fir tips. Reaching up, I picked a few buds for us to nibble on, and suggested we could make a wild soda from the fir tips and wild raspberries growing in abundance alongside the overgrown mountain footpaths. Coniferous soda is a simple drink I brew every year with the fir tips from my garden, and it was comforting to make it again, this time in Germany.

Back in England on a cold winter's day, ambling through a pine tree forest deep in the rolling hills of the Cotswolds, I looked up and saw pine resin – old and hardened like frosted amber on the trunk of one of the ancient trees. I gently harvested some from the bark, thinking about how this resin, when melted into skin-nourishing oils, would be the perfect antidote to wounds, old and new.

Coniferous soda is a simple drink I brew every year with the fir tips from my garden and it was comforting to make it again, this time in Germany.

Lilac blossom

Blossom

Aromatic spring blossom always fills my heart with joy. I could be anywhere in the world and the sight of lilac flowers would stop me in my tracks, inviting me closer to inhale their uplifting scent, leaving a powdery dusting on the tip of my nose as I lean in to greet them. Aside from its scent and delicate beauty, blossom enchants me because it is a physical reminder that re-awakening and blooming after harsh winters is inevitable, for us too. So much can change, but year after year, the blossom returns to delight and nourish us once more.

Blossom also boosts my confidence, believe it or not. Many spring days are spent building up the courage to ask neighbours and strangers if I can gather a few of their spring blooms.

Blossom tinctures, essences and cordials contain such simple ingredients that they can be made almost anywhere. From the hawthorn blossom that populates the hedgerows of the Yorkshire Dales, their stamens fleetingly appearing soft pink with pollen before they turn brown, to the delicate mimosa blossom that grows in the gardens of New Delhi. Then there is pomegranate blossom that flourishes in the foothills of the Atlas Mountains in Morocco, and the creamy elderflower blossom that tumbles down onto the pavements in the quiet back streets of London. Wherever we go, we can always find some blossom to enjoy in spring.

Making dandelion-infused honey

Weeds

I cherish finding familiar weeds and wildflowers when I visit new places. Weeds I come upon again and again are dandelions, pineapple weed and yarrow. So many medicinal weeds are trampled over without a second thought, and they invariably seem to be close by just when we need them.

On an anxiety-filled morning in Berlin, I found an abundance of pineapple weed growing alongside the path, as if it knew I could use its flowers for a nerve-soothing herbal tea. Yarrow is a herb I spot everywhere now too, thanks to a new foraging friend who identified it for me in Amsterdam. For this I am eternally grateful; yarrow is an incredible ally, alleviating my menstrual symptoms

and healing my skin that often becomes irritated in new climates.

Dandelions are a weed I am accustomed to making dandelion oil with, but I had been longing to find enough dandelions to make honey with their flowers. One summer in the French countryside, I stumbled upon an overgrown meadow that was an endless carpet of yellow dandelion sunshine. Gently picking the flower heads one by one, I could almost taste the dandelion honey, dripping off hot buttered toast fresh from the local boulangerie, all the while musing on how remarkable it was that one person's evil weed could be another person's melliferous treasure.

Tips for safe foraging

- Before touching, picking or eating a wild plant, you should be certain you know what it is. A lot of edible plants have poisonous look-alikes and mixing them up could have fatal consequences.
- The same plant that is suitable for me could cause a reaction in you, and I would strongly recommend you to seek advice from a health care professional before consuming a wild plant if you are pregnant, breastfeeding or on medication.
- Plant ID guides, foraging books and going out for walks with those knowledgeable on the subject will build your confidence in positively identifying plants.
- Watch out for areas that could be contaminated with animal faeces and pesticides.
- Remember that it is illegal to uproot any plant without the landowner's permission.
- Leave endangered plants alone and only pick from areas where the population of your chosen plant is plentiful, always leaving enough behind for the wild creatures and critters who depend on them.

With this in mind, I hope you feel inspired to do a little plant-seeking of your own and that you, too, will feel at home amongst the wild plants.

DORSET FLOWERS

Join us for a chat with herbalist Jemma Ricketts, who works with local farmers in Dorset, in the UK, to grow botanicals for a very special face oil. After carefully drying the herbs, they are infused in rapeseed oil that is pressed fresh on the farm.

*Photos by
Enchanted Plants*

Last year you launched your locally-grown botanical infused oil. Can you tell us more about this beautiful product that you've created?

It's the most exciting thing I've ever had the privilege to be part of. With the help of a couple of lovely farmers, we collectively grew a beautiful face oil from scratch! It contains 13 skin beneficial plant extracts – all grown, dried, pressed and infused in Dorset. The process has taught me a lot – as plants always do! I've connected with the weather and the soil, willed their growth, worried about them, marvelled at their beauty and strength – and ultimately watched all their hard work and ours turn into the most beautiful product.

I've always been passionate about plants and what they can do for us, which stems from my herbal medicine background. But increasingly, I've also become aware of some of the issues surrounding popular skin care ingredients that are on the market now, and how the latest trends can spark issues in the world. I feel that this project is a solution to these issues, where skin care ingredients benefit local communities and wildlife, instead of the reverse.

Can you tell us more about the issues surrounding some more exotic skin care ingredients?

There are many issues of sustainability in plant-based ingredients, especially as more and more people are choosing natural and organic plant-based food, skin care and lifestyles. Two of the most notable examples in recent times involve

frankincense and sandalwood plants, both of which are slow maturing plants and cannot be quickly replaced or easily farmed.

The level of frankincense tapping in Somalia to meet world demand has reached such a high level as to seriously threaten ancient wild desert plants and the local communities that have traditionally traded their resources and relied on those incomes for hundreds of years. As world prices rise for frankincense, particularly in the west with promises of anti aging skin care attributes, they tempt poor communities and ambitious companies to tap the frankincense trees beyond their ability to regenerate.

Equally, the hard wood Indian sandalwood trees have been hugely exploited in popular culture from use in joss sticks to shaving creams,

local, we can support our communities and there are many advantages for our environment, from travel and transport pollution, to sustainability of resources.

Some of the plants that you infused into your oil include calendula flowers, damask rose, lemon balm, yarrow, lavender, chamomile, comfrey, plantain, red clover, white clover, viola and bramble flower. How did you choose which plants to grow?

We chose plants that have multitasking skin benefits and of course plants that we could grow in the UK successfully and naturally. There are so many plants to choose from, but I was guided by my favourites and grew those that like to work together – plants do have friends they prefer to be with, at least they do in my mind!

I was also guided by the part of Dorset we are in and what flourishes here. This was particularly significant for some of the wild plants like bramble and plantain.

What is it like working with such fresh plants?

Well, in short, it has undermined every ingredient that I'd previously ever considered good – and I've sourced some really special organic ingredients in the past. I liken it to growing your own carrots. You pull them from the soil, cook them and then experience the freshest taste and fullest flavour which you can't compare to anything you've ever bought in a shop. I believe it comes down to the freshness and vibrancy of the natural ingredients. The herbs haven't

but responsible companies are under increasing pressure to provide sustainable options for both long term consumer demand and our increasing awareness of these environmental and social issues. Sustainable plantations have been created in Sri Lanka and Australia to help with the problem, which is a good start and they are developing sustainable supplies of frankincense in Oman among others. It's worth checking whenever you buy products with these ingredients.

It's always good to consider these aspects as we make decisions about where we buy our food or where our skin care comes from. Little changes can make a real difference to the pressure we put on our global environment. I think it remains the case that when we buy

experienced any of the degradation that can happen when plants travel.

Of course there is also the mental aspect to the process – in terms of the investment made between you and the plant. This does give a great level of satisfaction and appreciation.

Growing the plants was a beautiful collaboration between you and the farmers. What was it like working closely with the growers?

It was a new experience and one that has been so rewarding. I have learnt so much from the farmers and it has been a wonderful way of bringing together people and plants. Yordan, a Bulgarian national, worked in partnership with the landowner Justin, who comes from a heritage of natural medicine making and growing of medicinal plants. It was particularly lovely to share knowledge with them about how humans benefit from plants and the land.

I feel there is huge scope for developing the connection between

"...BY BUYING LOCAL WE CAN SUPPORT OUR COMMUNITIES AND THERE ARE MANY ADVANTAGES FOR THE ENVIRONMENT..."

local communities and the land and diversifying the usual agricultural produce to fulfil other needs.

What did you learn during the growing of the herbs? Were there any surprises?

Last summer was so hot and I was particularly worried about the more tender herbs like lemon balm and the damask roses. It was their first year of growth and I was concerned that they had not established enough of their root systems to cope with the heat and lack of rain. But, as usual, plants are so resourceful, so I needn't have worried. Also the soil had a good clay element which meant there was enough retained moisture to last for the many weeks of dry weather we experienced. Ironically as

I worried about the lack of rain, I started to read about the benefits of plants that are challenged in their natural environment. Plants actually increase their medicinal constituents in response to stresses and challenges and this can lead to the most beneficial of medicinal plants. I'm so glad we didn't panic and try to mass water!

One of the other delights was the incredible level of insects in the field. We can all imagine that flowers would attract many pollinators, but what I didn't expect were the hundreds of hornets over the yarrow as we were trying to harvest *(yarrow field shown in photo opposite)*. We were very respectful of each other, let's put it that way! I was also delighted to see a hummingbird hawk-moth. As the name suggests, it looked like a little hummingbird patrolling the lines of lavender. It was beautiful!

"PLANTS ACTUALLY INCREASE THEIR MEDICINAL CONSTITUENTS IN RESPONSE TO STRESSES AND CHALLENGES..."

Do you infuse the plants when dry?

Yes, I always infuse my herbs as dry as a crisp so the beneficial constituents are concentrated within the dried plant material. Also there is no risk the moisture levels turning the oil rancid.

Can you tell us more about the rapeseed oil that you use as a base?

The rapeseed, when cold pressed on the farm from the seed, has up to 30% vitamin E, whereas most comparable oils by the time they reach our formulation table have less than 10%. With less fresh oils, we often have to add vitamin E to help stabilise and preserve the oil. Whenever we need more rapeseed oil, we crush more of the stored seeds so the oil is always fresh.

Our rapeseed is a single variety of the plant with particularly high levels of vitamin K, which is very supportive to the antioxidant properties of our face oil. The rapeseed we use has significantly high levels of omega 3, 6 and 9 essential fatty acid compounds, which are wonderful for deep conditioning and natural moisture balance in the skin.

Do you plan to continue to grow and create more local products?

Yes, we have plans for growing and making a beautiful detoxifying daily cleansing oil next. Fingers crossed we can make it happen.

Visit *enchantedplants.co.uk* to find out more.

Jemma's botanical anointing oil recipe

Apply this anointing oil to your skin to give comfort and nourishment to both your body and spirit.

This is a simple recipe in the form of a herbal oil infusion. I've chosen some commonly available aromatic and therapeutic plants, some of which you may grow in your garden or know someone who does. There is particular magic in using plants that are fresh and grown by you or someone close.

The process of creating things with plants is often as therapeutic as using the end product. Then when you go to use your oil, give yourself a soothing temple massage at the same time. You've created this magical plant oil yourself and the therapy it will give to you will have so much meaning, not to mention the botanical benefits.

1. Find a clean jam jar or Kilner jar that seals well and is large enough to hold half of your oil and half of your herbs by volume.

2. Select a base oil – you need 100ml. Choose something vibrant such as a cold pressed olive oil or something grown and pressed locally, such as rapeseed oil, if this is local to you. Or choose a good quality sunflower or almond oil.

3. Collect your herbs – you need 25g in dried weight. I suggest equal parts of rosemary, lavender and rose petals. Take a few sprigs of each plant variety, and for the lavender - take some leaves as well as flowers. I'm a great believer in whole plants as the leaves help give the extracts a good balance. Choose your plants carefully: this is a special moment between you and your plants. Always thank the plant for its gift!

4. Spread your plants evenly on a clean tray and place somewhere dry and warm such as an airing cup-board or a window ledge in warmer weather. As soon as the plants feel crisp (and not rubbery in any way) they are ready.

5. Place the dried herb mixture into the bottom of your glass jar and pour enough oil over them to completely cover the herbs and give a little room for them to move in the oil. Try and fill your jar so that there is very little air in the top of the jar, as this will keep oxidation to a minimum.

6. The warmth and light of the sun can really enhance your infusion. The solar energy and warmth encourage the active constituents of the plants to transfer into the oil. Nurture your jar by placing it in the sun when it's sunny, and keep it cool and dark at night. The change in temperature along with the expansion and contraction of the plant material will make a beautifully active oil extract. Do this for three weeks and you will notice how the plant material softens as it absorbs the oil and how the oil colour changes as it takes on the colour of the plants.

7. At the end of the third week, strain your oil herb mixture through a muslin or similar. You can bottle your oil in dropper bottles and give as gifts or keep as a whole in another fresh jar. Label and date each one and they should last a whole year from straining date, if kept out of direct sunlight and heat. Amber or Miron violet glass will give best results for freshness. 🌿

tips

- Try to choose a pink rose – the darker pigments contain extra antioxidants.

- Drying rosemary when in flower is always a bonus.

- Add in some lavender leaves as well as flowers.

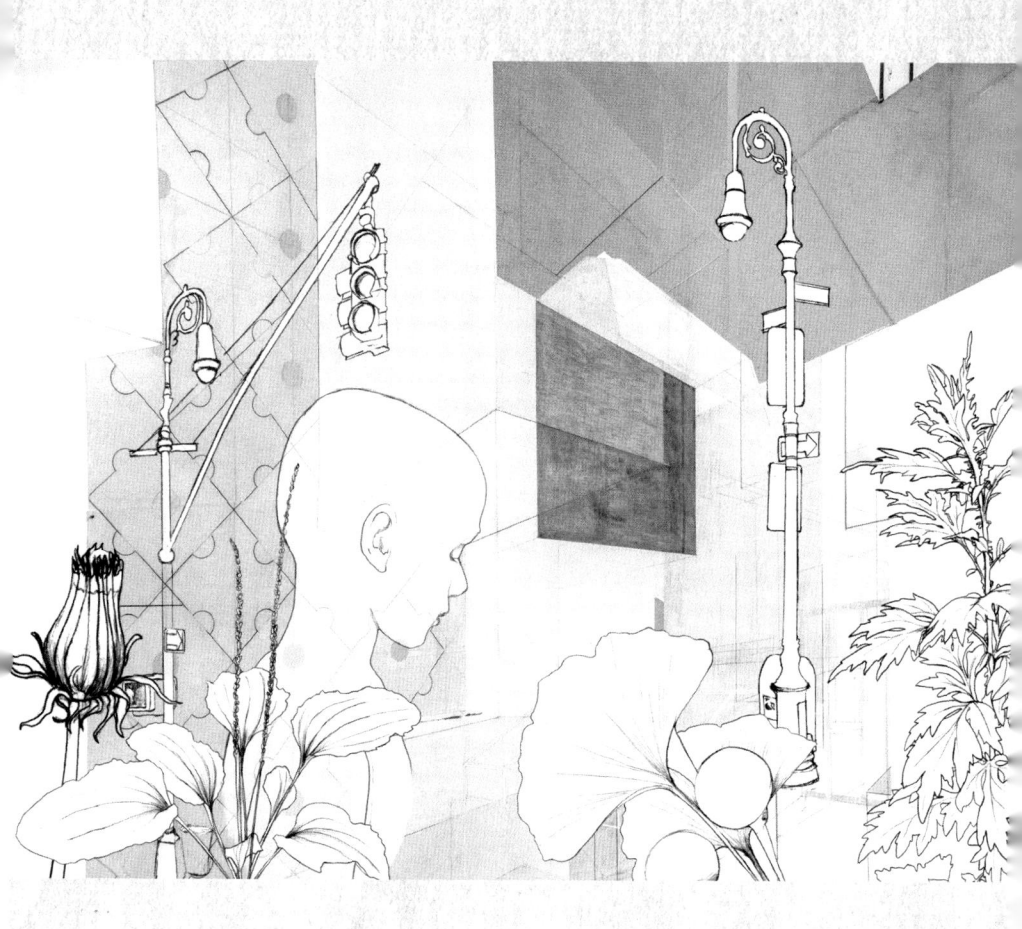

"PLANTS ARE OUR ALLIES AND
WANT TO TEACH US THEIR
SKILLS. [...] THE CONDITIONS OF
THE LAND HAVE AND ALWAYS
WILL REFLECT BACK WHAT WE
NEED FOR BALANCE."

URBAN TENDING

Words and illustrations by Alyssa Dennis

Herbalist and artist, Alyssa Dennis, tells us about the abundance of wild medicine that she has growing right outside her door.

What are the most familiar embodiments of home? Is it a place or a feeling? For most of us, home is where we rest, find comfort and safety, feel welcome and receive nourishment. Home is a sanctuary and space to cultivate togetherness and community. Outside of a modern Western mindset, home has also always been a place where local plants were made into food and medicine. An essential aspect of finding roots is understanding and honouring the traditional practices of those who came before us.

Traditional ecological knowledge of local plant medicine has been systematically stripped away first by the near decimation of indigenous peoples, coupled with both the legalities made against this medicine and those who worked with it to support and heal their own communities. In the last century, the commodification of our basic necessities in the name of convenience has seduced us away from a common understanding in the virtues and efficacy of local plant medicine. Yet, having autonomy and agency around your own health and wellness is to be home.

In many cultures around the world, it is still commonplace for communities of about 100 people or so to have a local shaman, herbalist, plant whisperer or curandero who operates as healer by way of fully integrating and studying every plant within a 50 to 100-mile radius. This kind of engagement with our surroundings has defined the very foundation we stand on and has helped to characterize the origins of culture itself. I was astounded to realize that within just a one block radius of my apartment in Brooklyn, New York, there are nearly 20 wild species that have been used as food and medicine. Yet in urban, suburban and rural areas we denigrate, devalue, destroy, down play and dig out this bounty in favour of expensive exotic cultivars, monocrops and pesticide-dependent green lawns.

"...THE REMEDY FOR WHAT CURRENTLY AILS YOU IS A PLANT THAT GROWS RIGHT OUTSIDE YOUR DOOR."

Herbalists often talk about how the remedy for what currently ails you is a plant or host of plants that grow right outside your door. How is this possible? The genius of plants is that they thrive in areas that require their honed abilities. Plants are a product of their environment just as we are. Calling on their millions of years of experience, they are intelligent barometers, a mirrored reflection of how the ecosystem is challenged by human influences or otherwise.

For example, *Ginkgo biloba* is one the most common tree species planted by the City of New York to line its streets. Its leaves are prized by herbalists to *"improve circulation and oxygen metabolism"* (K.P. Kalsa). Ginkgo is a native to China and the Chinese have been harvesting the seeds for thousands of years to moisten and treat imbalances of the lungs. In fact, the two-lobed leaves resemble our two bilaterally lobed organs: the brain and the lungs! Its use as a lung remedy is fascinating when you consider that this species has been found in the fossils record dating back 270 million years (gingko being the only species left from the *Ginkgophyta* family) which means it evolved in an atmosphere with much less oxygen than we have now. This is why it does so well in oxygen-poor, smog-filled urban areas like NYC. Although I am not promoting the further use of fossil fuels, ginkgo has mastered these environmental restraints and can help us do the same. In addition to the herb's terpene lactones constituents: ginkgolides and bilobalides that protect our nerve cells and improve circulation, gingko also prevents cell damage by free radicals.

Ginkgo biloba

Another example of plant intelligence in a human-dominated environment is plantain. *Plantago major* is a low-growing species with several wide-shaped leaves growing in a basal rosette. It thrives in dry, damaged compacted soil. Native peoples often called it *"white-man's footsteps"* because wherever Europeans developed hardened paths or roads, the plantain would appear. Although plantain grows in dry, disturbed places, it has mastered surviving in these conditions while maintaining exceptionally moist skin. Their seeds can take on nine times their weight in water. Its leaves are rounded without any irritating hairs or spikes and have a hardy, pliable thickness. Plantain's many virtues include aerating and depositing nutrients into the soil. Unsurprisingly, this species happily finds its home among nutrient poor, dry concrete jungles. Plantain contains a substance called mucilage which acts to coat and sooth irritated skin. This species also has astringent and antibacterial qualities that help tighten and tone the skin while preventing infection. Just as plantain is a healer of the earth's wounds, it is also an internal and external remedy for the surface wounds of the human body.

Yes! Plants are magic! Just think of all the other millions of species across this planet and what they've mastered that we haven't. Plants are our allies and want to teach us their skills. They are our ancient ancestral mentors just as the indigenous peoples who mastered the language and decoding of these plants are also our teachers. The conditions of the land have and always will reflect back what we need for balance. Once we're

Plantago major

able to perceive this reflection, locality becomes important not simply from the perspective of a low carbon footprint but as a paradigm shift in how we live within our environment. To receive these gifts, we must turn our ears to the ground and humbly lower ourselves.

We must take caution in connecting with plants that are exposed to contamination, especially in urban areas. Certain plants bioaccumulate heavy metal toxins which will transfer to us by ingesting them. This is a reality that we must address head on and I am not advocating that we pick any plant without the advice of a trained professional. But this risk also points to an important truth. If we truly understood the magnificent abundance of viable food and medicine within our own surroundings, we would see pollution and pesticide use as a direct assault against our own freedom of finding place and truly be home.

If the plants that grow around us are healthy enough to harvest, we must learn, as indigenous people do, to work in direct stewardship with the land. When this is done, there is little room for looting, clearing or stripping away of resources. People do not inherently strip their own community dry - they cultivate it. Enacting a clearing, taking, or hoarding of the earth's bounty, whether we are "from" that particular place or not, shows we are not truly home. We have suffered through a vicious cycle of this mentality since Europeans set foot on what they thought was a "New World."

To find better footing and live in stewardship with the land is to learn the practices of tending. Tending *"reestablishes the ecological associations between people and nature"* (M. Cat Anderson). It is *"…the product of keen observation, patience, experimentation,*

and long-term relationships with plants and animals. It is knowledge built on a history, gained through many generations of learning passed down by elders..." It has been proven time and again that the more one is able to tend their surroundings, the more resources there will be. Unfortunately, humans are among the only beings on the planet that don't consistently tend the environment they inhabit. The problem is we don't have a well-seasoned approach to regenerative practices that cultivate nature through reciprocity. Although we are beginning to see the merits of regenerative practices, in very small pockets, we by-in-large exist outside of this way of thinking.

Perhaps the beneficial experience of walking in a forest, spending the day at the park or acquiring a potted plant is not just about breathing in fresh oxygen, but experiencing joy at feeling the plants calling us back to having a relationship with them. For centuries we have dangerously positioned nature as an abstraction of something to leave alone, exploit or visit as an outsider. We ought to heed the wisdom of our great plant teachers because extensive environmental degradation, soil depletion and the consequential decline in physical, mental and emotional health tell us we can no longer turn a blind eye. Indigenous people believe that when you consume your local environment, you become one with it and it strengthens the foundation on which you stand to move forward in life. Tending and finding nourishment from the wild is an absolute necessity for rooting to home. 🌿

"TENDING AND FINDING NOURISHMENT FROM THE WILD IS AN ABSOLUTE NECESSITY FOR ROOTING TO HOME."

References

- Anderson, M Kat. *Tending the Wild: Native American Knowledge and the Management of California's Natural Resources*. University of California Press. 2015.
- Khalsa, KP. *Ginkgo Biloba Benefits*. Sept. 1, 2011.

LADY FERN

The Wondersmith gifts free surprise sensory experiences to lucky strangers. In these magical events, everything is carefully designed to give a real taste of the place.

Words by The Wondersmith and photos by Mike Bragg

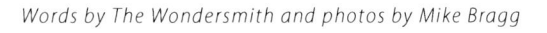

Home is the smell of damp moss and pine needles. Home is the feeling of bare feet sinking into soft earth. Home is the sound of chick-a-dees. Home is the flavour of wild violets or huckleberries. Home is believing in fairytales.

All my life I have been exploring what "home" means to me and how I can share that beauty with others. The main guiding word for my artwork is "terroir," which loosely translates to "the taste of a place." More specifically, this word is used in describing all of the variables that make something taste a specific way, from plant variety to geology to cultural traditions. I like to think of terroir as encompassing even more than that, though. To me, it means capturing a specific time and place, a magical moment, whether through natural dyes harvested at my friend's homestead that I use to dye my tablecloths, the barnacles clinging to rocks on my favourite beach that inspire so many of my ceramic pieces, or a feast of foraged plants gathered from the woods I love to wander in.

Allow me to introduce myself: I am Miss Wondersmith. I call myself that because I work with 'wonder' as more than just inspiration; it has become a core ingredient in the artwork I create. I explore the themes of both 'terroir' and 'wonder' by designing immersive gatherings based on the natural beauty of my region, then gift them to strangers. I first decide on what I'd like each gathering to "gift" to my guests, from wild exploration to a reflective conversation. Then, I come up with a creative way to attract the kind of guests that will appreciate the experience. From messages-in-a-bottle left on the shores of winter beaches to attract poetic wanderers, to invitations tucked into self-help books to reach those looking for a conversation about change, these strangers are rewarded for their curiosity with an experience they will not soon forget.

While this story may conjure up thoughts of fairy tales, it's something that really happened not too long ago in the magical woods of coastal Oregon. I created this magical gathering on a whim, not knowing at the time that it would completely shape both my art practice and my life. Today, I still hold onto the wonder of that evening as I plan and create other such magical gatherings.

I always look to nature for the inspiration for my events. My home region is just bursting with amazing natural sights and plentiful plants to forage! I find my time in the woods to be grounding and centering, and creative inspiration often comes while I'm in this most natural of homes. When I'm designing a gathering, I consider every aspect from the tableware and setting to the food and the ceremony. I handcraft the vessels we will dine from out of glass or ceramic, decorating them with glazes that mimic rainforest greens or delicate forms inspired by tidepools. I often use nature as my backdrop, and have been known to hike miles with a heavy pack full of glass pieces and food to set up a feast in the middle of the woods. Finally, I infuse each gathering with a ceremony based on the structure of a good story. From the call-to-adventure of finding an invitation in a public setting to the (often physical) threshold crossing into a new world, I give my guests an escape from the ordinary, a love letter to the region that all of us call home.

Imagine you are walking through a mossy rainforest when you spot a purple fern sprouting amongst a cluster of green ones. This anomaly intrigues you, so you venture over to it to investigate further. On the fern is a mysterious invitation to a dinner party, held by someone known only as 'Lady Fern.' You accept the invitation and show up to a feast under a canopy of fairy lights and sparkling crystalized seedpods. On a table laden with handmade glass and ceramic dishes, you are served a feast of vibrant foods foraged from those very same woods, washed down with a good helping of magic. Something about sharing this experience with a handful of other lucky strangers feels like coming home; not in a physical sense, but in a soul-sense.

Before I became Miss Wondersmith, I created private events, usually funded

through ticket sales. My aims then were similar – to share wonder and an appreciation for the natural beauty of my home with my guests, but I soon began to feel that something about them wasn't right. Charging admission removed the magic from the experience and turned my artwork into just another social resume-padding experience for the elite few that could afford them. Instead of engaging with the experience itself, I saw many of my guests more concerned with taking photos to show off to their friends later. After one last event that left me feeling deflated, I created Lady Fern's Soirée on a whim. I used artwork I had already created and foraged most of the food myself, keeping my costs minimal. I held it in my own backyard and stuck those purple ferns along my favourite hiking trails, just to see what would happen.

"...I GIVE MY GUESTS AN ESCAPE FROM THE ORDINARY, A LOVE LETTER TO THE REGION THAT ALL OF US CALL HOME."

What happened was a gathering like nothing I'd ever experienced before. The guests that came were absolutely delighted with what I had prepared for them. They were engaged in excited conversations with each other for the entire evening. The diversity of personalities and backgrounds was electrifying – a mix of 20-somethings, older parents with young children, and retirees, all brought together through the shared experience of stumbling upon a magical invitation in the woods. My favorite part of the event was seeing all of their reactions to it. Two young women showed up and informed me that, for some strange reason, they had imagined I would have horses decorated with ribbons. A retired couple told me that they'd been looking for this kind of magic for years, and had cried when they'd stumbled upon my invitation in the woods. But the best reaction was that of the three young children that attended. I had expected them to be the most excited, but instead their attitude was more like, *"of course we're at a fairy picnic, duh, Dad."* It was a hilarious comparison to the awe-struck wonder of the 20-somethings in our midst.

Inviting strangers changed the dynamic of the evening completely. Instead of a familiar group with stale conversations, I was seeing a diverse group of people bond over a shared magical experience. I was watching a community form, right before my very eyes. And I got to be part of it!

When the guests had said their last goodbyes, the dishes had been cleared, and the darkness of a spring evening had settled over the town, I sat in reflection under those twinkling seedpods with eyes brimming with tears of gratitude. It was in those moments that I made the decision: this is what I am meant to do. I resolved to continue giving these free and immersive experiences to strangers, no matter what.

"THE BEST WAY TO FIND MORE MAGIC IN THE WORLD IS TO MAKE IT YOURSELF."

To cover my costs, I turned to crowdfunding and set up an account on the website Patreon *(patreon.com/thewondersmith)*, where others who were inspired by my work could support me with a small monthly contribution. As word spread about what I was doing, those little donations added up to become a fund I can now pull from whenever I want to share some more magic with strangers.

It's taken a lot of perseverance and no small amount of passion to get here, but today I am happy to say that I am able to dedicate my life to fulfilling the goals I set on that memorable night. I am still creating wild gatherings and sharing them with strangers. In addition, I'm also spreading wonder through my blog, where I write about foraged recipes, everyday magic, and rituals or ceremonies meant to foster connection and community.

If this article can leave you with one thing, let it be this: the best way to find more magic in the world is to make it yourself. Anyone can create wonder and give it to others, whether that is writing encouraging notes and leaving them in public places or hosting magical gatherings for your family and friends. All it takes is a little imagination and creativity.

A note about safety: I've taken my own safety and the safety of my guests into serious consideration with each event I create. I always host events with friends or volunteers, and I have every guest RSVP with their full names, a little bit about themselves, and a list of any allergies or intolerances I should be aware of. In addition, everyone attending signs a liability waiver and I make sure to keep these gatherings in public spaces where help could be quickly accessed should anything go wrong. I would recommend anyone interested in expanding their social circle to first reach out to groups they are already a part of such as book clubs, classmates, or team mates!

Purple Pansy Salad Rolls

These delicious and healthy treats are jam-packed with the magic of purple vegetables. A variety of flavours and textures keeps them interesting; sour-sweet cabbage slaw, crunchy sprouts, creamy avocado, soft and fluffy sweet potatoes, and crisp carrots keeps them dynamic while fresh violets and pansies dress them up to be worthy of any fairy gathering. To make them even more delightful, serve them with the purple velvet dipping sauce!

Purple is a special colour indeed. It's associated with both spirituality and royalty. It brings to mind luxury, magic and wisdom. The pigments found in most naturally-occurring purple foods are called anthocyanins. These water-soluble pigments can appear red, purple, blue or black. Their name comes from the Greek words for both "flower" and "dark blue," which is appropriate considering two of my favourite sources are wild violets and blueberries! Anthocyanins are a type of flavonoid, which are a powerful family of antioxidants.

To make approx. 12 rolls:

- 2 cups finely sliced red cabbage
- 1 tbsp lemon juice
- ¼ tsp salt
- ¼ cup currants
- 4-5 finely sliced purple carrots
- 1 medium purple sweet potato
- 2 tbsp olive oil
- 1 ripe avocado
- 1 cup sprouts
- 2 cups wild greens (I used dandelion & mallow)
- 12 rice paper sheets
- Fresh violets & pansies (5 per roll)

1. Combine the cabbage, lemon juice, salt and currants in a medium bowl. Knead for about 2 minutes to soften the cabbage, then let sit while you prepare the rest of the components.

2. Preheat oven to 400 F (200 °C). Meanwhile, peel the purple sweet potato and cut into small slices. Toss in oil and sprinkle with salt and spread on a parchment-lined baking sheet. Roast the sweet potatoes for 10-15 minutes or until tender.

3. Slice the avocado and cut the carrots into small matchsticks. Wash the wild greens and shake dry. Lay out all of the components, plus a plate to roll on and a shallow dish of warm water.

4. Place a rice paper sheet into the water and let soak until soft (about 40 seconds). Gently remove it and spread it on the plate. Add a little of each mixture (cabbage salad, purple carrots, sweet potatoes, sprouts, avocado, and wild greens), then fold up the ends to overlap the fillings slightly. Roll tightly one full rotation.

5. Stick a few edible flowers on the roll and finish rolling all the way to the end of the rice paper. The flowers should be underneath 1 layer of wrapper, sitting between the top layer and the second layer that holds in the filling.

6. Repeat the process until you run out of fillings only soaking 1 wrapper at a time (soak 1 while you roll 1). Keep the completed rolls under a damp towel to stay moist while you prepare the rest.

To make the purple velvet sauce:

- two thirds of a cup of blueberries
- ½ cup cashew nuts, presoaked
- ½ cup basil and mint leaves (approx. equal proportion - use purple basil for deeper colour)
- 2 tbsp sumac + 1 cup water or 3 tbsp. lemon juice
- ½ tsp salt
- 2 fresh garlic cloves, minced
- 1 tbsp olive oil
- ½ tbsp nutritional yeast
- 1 tbsp sriracha pepper sauce (optional)

Boil the water and add the sumac to infuse and let sit for about 20 minutes, then strain. Then add ½ cup sumac tea to a blender (or 3 tbsp. lemon juice if you don't have sumac), along with all the other ingredients. Blend until smooth. Assess the flavour and consistency and add more sumac tea (or lemon juice) as needed to add more tartness. If the mixture is tart enough but too thick, just add a little water and blend again until it reaches the consistency you like. 🌿

PETAL PAINT

Explore your local flowers by turning the
petals into watercolour paints.

Words and photo by Rebecca Desnos

This is such a simple and beautiful way to sample local dye colours. All you need is hot water and a little bowl. If you take a thermos flask of hot water, you can even do this when you're outside in nature and paint on the go! I've used dried flowers from my African violet house plant, as well as marigolds and coreopsis from my balcony. This technique works best with deeply pigmented flowers.

What you need:

- Flowers (fresh or dried)
- A few little bowls (do not use for food again afterwards) or little jars with lids (helpful when travelling).
- A stick
- Lemon juice
- Bicarbonate of soda (baking soda)
- Paintbrushes
- Paper for painting
- Optional: sieve and paint palette

Let's make our paint!

1. Take the petals off a few deeply pigmented flowers and drop into a bowl or glass jar. Pour a little hot water over the petals – just enough so the petals are covered. Mix well with the stick (or the end of a paintbrush) and try to squash the petals to extract more colour. Leave for a little while to allow the colour to darken.

2. When you're happy with the depth of colour, you can just dip your brush into the liquid and begin painting. Or strain out the petals to leave a clear paint that's free of any petals.

3. The dye from petals is sometimes pH sensitive, so pour a little dye into a couple of the wells in a paint palette (or extra bowls) and add a squeeze of lemon juice (or vinegar) to one, and a sprinkle of bicarbonate of soda to another. If the dye is pH sensitive, the colours are likely to change immediately. As you paint, rinse your paintbrush between dips so you don't 'contaminate' the pH of each liquid.

Please take care when identifying flowers and ensure that they are not toxic. Also, note that the colours from some flowers will last longer than others, so bare this in mind when creating art. To paint fabric, follow the methods on pages 88-95 for pretreating fabric and heat-setting the dye. 🌿

African Violet

African Violet + lemon

African Violet + baking soda

Coreopsis

Coreopsis + lemon

Coreopsis + baking soda

Red Marigold

Safety: Please ensure you correctly identify flowers before eating.

EDIBLE FLOWERS

Bex Partridge shares some tips for growing and using
edible flowers. Grow them on your windowsills or in
your garden, and enjoy their eye-popping colour in
your dishes and baking!

Words and photos by Bex Partridge

Did you know that edible flowers don't just add colour and texture to our meals? They can also add delicate flavours. For example, nasturtiums have a peppery aftertaste which makes them a tasty addition to summer salad. Calendula petals have a slightly citrus taste which compliments their bright hues.

My appreciation of edible flowers started many years ago when I worked as a full time chef. After I left catering college, I took a job at an events company and worked for a wonderful lady who grew many of her own herbs and edible flowers. We used these botanicals to decorate and add flavour to the dishes we were serving. This was over 15 years ago; back then she was a trail blazer of sorts, although at the time I didn't see it!

Even now I'm still amazed by the number of edible flowers that exist. Many of them are flowers that you probably already know and are perhaps already growing in your garden, such as pansies and

violas. When I use flowers in my cooking or baking, I love to use a multitude of different varieties and colours. To me, there's nothing more pleasing than a salad adorned with a rainbow of flowers.

Some of the easiest ways to use edible flowers is to decorate salads and other dishes with them. Simply sprinkle a salad with calendula petals or the pretty little faces of violas just as you are about to serve. If you love to cook, you can press them into homemade pasta or sprinkle them on top of a meringue. Or press the flowers and use them to decorate the sides of cakes. The possibilities are endless.

My favourite way has to be on botanical biscuits. I start with a base slightly spiced with crushed pink peppercorns, then gently press the flowers on the top of the cookies before I slide them into the oven. When cooked, the flowers will turn softer, muted tones but they still add an extra touch to your bakes.

calendula, pansy,
viola, nasturtium (in the
hand), as well as fennel
and dill leaves to add an
aniseed flavour and a hint
of green!

Tips for growing

Space

The brilliant thing about most of the edible flowers that I have spoken about here is that you don't need a huge amount of space to grow them. A few pots on a porch or balcony, or even in a window box, is all you really need. Flowers that do particularly well in pots are violas and pansies. Nasturtiums can also thrive in small spaces and the trailing varieties add beauty to walls.

Sowing your seeds

Seeds can be started off on a warm window ledge where they have enough light and warmth to germinate. A tray filled with seed compost will do perfectly – this compost is finer than most and ensures the seeds don't get swamped. Sprinkle a packet of seeds over the top, give them a gentle water, then wait for the green shoots to appear. Once they are a good size, with at least two sets of leaves, rehouse the seedlings into bigger flower pots. Gently tease out the strongest of your seedlings and transfer them to a larger pot. Seeds sown in spring can then be put outside when all danger of frost has passed.

Maintaining your plants

The magical truth about edible flowers (as a general rule) is that they are of the *cut-and-come-again* variety. This means that by picking the flowers, we encourage the growth of more. Essentially, what we are doing is stopping the flowers from going to seed. When a plant starts to go to seed, it puts all of its energy into this process, setting itself up for the next year. But we can prolong the flowering period by regularly picking flower heads once they have bloomed. And when the season is over and your plants are getting a little scraggly, you can then let them to go to seed and collect seeds for next year so you can begin the cycle again.

Serving + eating your flowers

Clean thoroughly

Inspect for any lurking bugs. Earwigs, for example, love to live in the back horn part of a nasturtium flower, and the deep petals of calendula can house small beetles. Make sure you give your blooms a good once over before you serve them.

Pick in advance

Edible flowers can be gathered before they are needed and stored in the fridge for a few days. Keep them in a pot with a damp piece of kitchen paper underneath to retain freshness.

Baking botanical biscuits

Add fresh flowers onto your favourite shortbread or biscuits before baking. Gently place the flowers on, then put a sheet of greaseproof paper on top of the flower and roll with a rolling pin. This helps keep the flowers flat rather than curling up - and sometimes entirely off - the biscuit.

Just keep in mind that when baking flowers in the oven, colours are likely to lose some of their vibrance as the flowers dry out in the heat.

Photo of baked biscuits by Lulu Peddar

"Keep close to Nature's heart... and break clear away, once in a while, and climb a mountain or spend a week in the woods. Wash your spirit clean".

— John Muir

REWILDING

Walk barefoot to help your body align with
the natural heartbeat of the earth.

Words and photo by Louise Gale

Rewilding is essentially a term used
to bring something back to its natural
state. It is a term most often used with
landscapes and places, but is now being
introduced as a concept to help us
reconnect ourselves with nature and,
most importantly, to give ourselves
permission to be away from technology.

Are you someone who is constantly
ensuring your mobile devices are
charged? Imagine if you recharged your
own energy system as often as you find
yourself charging your mobile devices.
How grounded and connected do you
think you would feel to the natural world
around you?

One thing I give myself permission to do
every day is to touch the earth with my
bare feet, wherever I find myself. To me,
it is a way to connect with the energy
of the place I find myself in and balance
and recharge my own energy system—
especially if I can place my bare feet on
grass, sand, the dirt or in water.

Grounding or Earthing (in an electrical-
power sense) is all about removing the
excess charge of an object. Think of
yourself as this object. Grounding is a
process that helps the body connect to
earth energies—specifically the electrons
that are naturally part of our planet. In
this modern world, buzzing with invisible
waves and technology, we are in greater
need to connect with the earth, get rid
of that excess charge and feel grounded.

When we touch the ground or connect
with nature, the earth's electrons are
conducted to our body, bringing us
closer in tune with the earth itself, and
its tranquil energy naturally transfers to
us when we are in it.

Our body aligns with the pulse and the natural heartbeat of the earth (also known as the Schumann Resonance which vibrates at around 7.83 Hz, but has been seen to be rising in recent years!). This frequency was found to be the same as the frequency of our brain in its natural state. Many discoveries have been made that this resonance is essential to our physical and mental wellbeing.

Walking barefoot will get rid of the build up of any electrical stress caused by being surrounded by all of our electronic devices! It helps keep our immune system intact by providing our body with these much needed electrons and natural frequencies.

Direct body contact with the earth or ocean (water is naturally conducting) can discharge static electricity from your body. Inviting nature back into our busy lives is essential. If we can create space to ensure this is part of our daily lives, we will lead a much more balanced, happy and fulfilling life. Nature is all around us; even in a busy city we can find sanctuary in a local park or courtyard garden. No matter where you are in the world, you can connect earth's energy through the soles of your feet. 🌿

Excerpt from Louise Gale's book *Botanical Mandalas: Draw, Paint and Create Expressive Mandalas Inspired by Nature* (2018).

RECONNECTING

Join us for a chat with Sophie Parker who runs
Betony & Sage. We talk about reconnecting with nature,
foraging responsibly and making conscious choices to
reduce our impact on the planet.

Photos by Sophie Parker

Hi Sophie, it's lovely chatting to you. Can you tell us a bit about yourself and what you do?

I started Betony and Sage at the end of 2017 with the aim of creating natural products that are gentle on our planet and also to inspire others to reconnect with the natural world.

At a time when so many of us feel removed from nature, I try to show others that nature is not something outside of us, but within us. Nature is our life support machine – she provides us with the water we drink and the air we breathe, the fibres on our backs and the wonderment we find in beautiful places.

I have worked in environmental conservation for 10 years and still work as a ranger for a conservation charity, but my passion is *connection* – with others

and with nature. This is why I started Betony & Sage – to encourage others to slow down, seek balance and most of all, to help others foster a connection with mother nature and a desire to protect her.

We are facing many challenges due to the unsustainable nature of our consumerist society with species extinction rates greater than ever before. But we can reduce our impact on the world by making conscious decisions about what we buy and researching the ingredients in our products.

You create a gorgeous range of relaxing aromatherapy candles. Is creating a sense of calm and comfort important to you?

In short, yes. My aim is to produce organic and wild-crafted products that

can help others slow down, take stock and create a little balance in our fast-paced world. For me, lighting a candle is a real marker of slowing down; the soft light, the flickering flame, along with scents that can awaken memories and support our emotions. All of this can offer us comfort – a feeling of snugness and warmth. It is during these moments of slowness that we have time to reflect and discover our true essence. It gives us time to create our own magic.

Can you tell us more about the ingredients in your products and your choices behind them?

The ingredients I use in my products are incredibly important to me. From the base oils I use, to the glass jars I house my products in, thought goes into every element.

I like to use wild-sourced ingredients

"I AM KEEN TO ENSURE THAT FORAGING FOR INGREDIENTS DOES NOT HAVE A NEGATIVE IMPACT ON WILDLIFE."

wherever possible. As a conservationist, I am keen to ensure that foraging for ingredients does not have a negative impact on wildlife. For example, when I forage for rosehips for my facial oil, I will only take a small amount from any one place, ensuring that hips remain for the birds to overwinter on.

I choose to use organic ingredients; from organic essential oils to organic dried flowers that rest in my salt soaks and on the tops of my candles. In many circumstances, chemical input in farming occurs at such high levels and we are only just beginning to understand the impact that these chemicals have on our wildlife. For example, we now know the impact that neonicotinoids have on bees – an insect vital for the pollination of many of the plants we eat and utilise. The EU banned the use of these chemical pesticides in 2018, thankfully.

When it came to candle making, I spent almost a year researching the wax I would use. Originally, I decided on an organic wax blend. Unfortunately, I soon discovered that one component of the wax was palm oil. At the moment it is very difficult to ensure that palm oil is responsibly sourced, so I made the decision to not use it. I began to search for an alternative. I wanted to use a plant-based wax that grew in the UK to reduce the air miles associated with my candles. The only natural wax that I could find that is grown and processed in the UK is rapeseed wax. After much research and product trials, my decision was made and my candles are now made using this crop. A lot of consideration has gone into this, and still does. I am aware

that rapeseed is a brassica and therefore it is difficult to grow organically. It is however a crop used by birds and insects whilst it is grown. Also as it is grown and produced here in the UK, I can be more assured of the regulations around crop farming and environmental laws and considerations that come into play. It is incredibly important to me that my products genuinely have a low environmental impact.

What does self care mean to you personally?

Self care is really important to me. Like so many of us, I am always trying to balance the different aspects of my life and it can sometimes feel overwhelming.

When I make time for myself and pause for a moment, my true feelings step forward and I can clearly look at what is bringing me joy and what I am finding challenging.

Time outdoors is a vital form of self care for me. The profound beauty that can be found in the most simple natural objects brings so much joy to my heart – the structure of a pine cone, the movement of water down a stream, the noise of a blackbird singing at dusk. These things make my heart sing with glee.

Alongside walks with nature, an important form of my self care is taking time to journal. Writing down my thoughts helps me to clear my head

and stops me worrying that I will forget something I want to hold on to. There is something powerful about letting thoughts flow out and then finding something beautiful on the page afterwards.

After I have journalled, I like to use locally sourced herbs to cleanse the space. One of my favourites is cedar. I gather windfall from the area of land I look after, but waiting for this wise old tree to drop a branch can take some time. Working at mother nature's pace teaches us patience and shows the true beauty of seasonality.

Can you tell us about some of your favourite essential oil blends?

Many of my candle blends were chosen because the aroma reminded me of a particular moment in nature. I do have a couple of personal favourites; lavender reminds me of my grandmother who used to keep dried bundles around her home. Every time I put lavender into my smudge sticks I am reminded of her, of her positivity and the sunshine she brought into my life.

As well as using dried lavender, I really enjoy blending an organic lavender essential oil with clove or a spice such as cardamom. For me, it feels like a relaxing and nurturing scent – almost like a hug.

This year I have really connected with rosemary. It is such a powerful herb – just rubbing her leaves between my fingers gives me energy and uplifts me. I enjoy using rosemary with orange as an uplifting blend that's perfect for mornings.

You organise local gatherings and nature retreats. Can you tell us more about these?

I would say that in my most natural way of being, I am very much an introvert! However, there is real magic in connecting with others and helping them find joy and pleasure in plants and nature.

I feel very honoured to have been able to facilitate 'wow' moments in nature for other people. In my work as a ranger, I have spent many days showing children and adults the wonders inside a rock pool or traditional skills like making charcoal. Those moments when you see someone connect with nature, the switch flicks and they are transfixed by the creature under the log or the dragonfly larvae in the pool. Those moments are what really light me up. I realise that by sharing my passion with others, I am enabling others to reconnect with Mother Nature and their own wild soul.

I qualified as a forest school practitioner in 2015 and have enjoyed creating gatherings for others to explore the outdoors, to build self-esteem and to showcase some of the natural wonders all around us. For me alone, my passion for the natural world is doing some good, but along with others, we can change the world. This year I hope to run a series of wild woman workshops. It is something I am really excited about after hosting wild-crafting walks last year. 🌿

"WORKING AT MOTHER NATURE'S PACE TEACHES US PATIENCE AND SHOWS THE TRUE BEAUTY OF SEASONALITY."

MOTHERING
PLANTS

"I ask their permission before taking a leaf in hand..."

Words and photo by Ocean Rose Fashakin

I wake up before the music of the day has begun. It's still very early; the peach morning light is just starting to filter in through the linens. A golden symphony. I can hear them gently bend, stretch, drip and exhale in unison. I ask their permission before taking a leaf in hand then brush away dust. Life has been happening. Here. I realise someone has been singing; I've been humming to the plants as we exchange life. This is home. Us. The pressure of reality awaits just after day breaks, but this is made infinitely more manageable following these sweet moments. Managing time. Mothering plants.

The place where a pot used to be feels colossal, even if only for a moment when a plant drinks the rain or shower water. Revived and refreshed. The space has now been replaced by a terracotta pot, still patchy from its watering. Dripping nourishment. The leaves glimmering as a small thank you. Radical kindness.

As I leave home for the school run, I pack away these feelings – neatly tuck them into a pocket. Mine and little one's. Sometimes balled up and dropped in a bag, only to be ironed out and eased in a place of calm and tranquillity. Knowing the plants await our movements gives me immense joy. They are robust in a delicate way – able to withstand the enthusiastic yet gently innocent hands of a five year old. A symbiotic exchange.

I think about what spirit I have yet to see them in; does it transform into a kaleidoscope of ever changing light when we are not home? Can the feeling

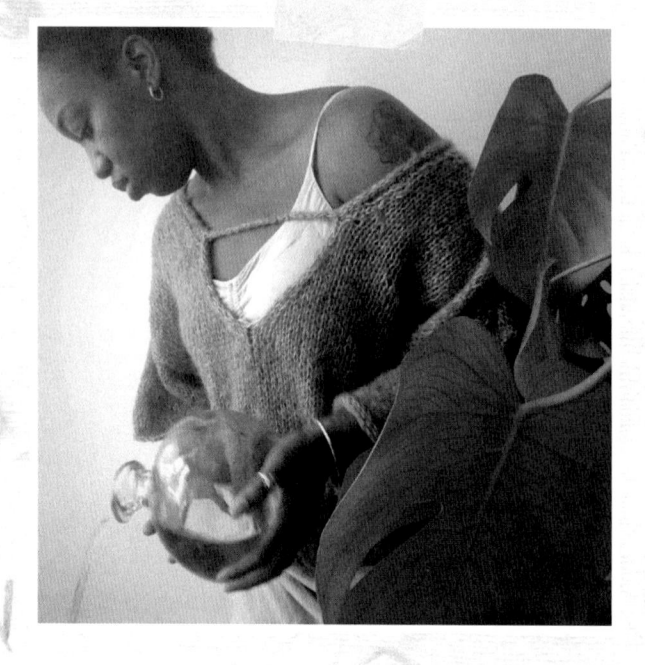

be slipped into a neat space between heart and hand, forever present and eagerly waiting to help ease those heavy feelings, knitting them into a fabric for life?

We were without a home at one point – between street and shelter – floating through a city of untimely changes. Life felt greyer than usual without our familiar green escape. We gathered our belongings into a worn pocket – with a single succulent leaf, home was closer than I'd previously thought.

The realisation came in waves. Home could be propagated and taken with us, even in the most minute ways. The feelings. The thoughts. We welcomed this closeness to plants with an open embrace. To be.

The tenderness so closely connected with plants can be found wherever these green-growers are: in the wild, where they are undeniably alluring in an unassuming way, to that curated aesthetic that can only be found only in a city boutique. Both allow for a vast range of people to find what sparks that intimacy that only plants can give. Life.

Whether they trail and caress our face as we pass by, or require a more concentrated glance, plants are little reminders to value and appreciate seemingly empty spaces. My shelf that was once occupied by a book passed on by a friend is now filled by a small pot of a slow-growing green – a new addition to the family. I am reminded to take it easy and that we all have room to grow. Home. 🌿

AYURVEDA IN THE HOME

How to use ayurveda to balance our
inner & outer homes.

Words by Naina Bajaria

According to ayurveda, we all have a constitution. This is called our **prakruti** which is a unique combination of the elements that display particular characteristics within our mental and physical body. As soon as we are conceived, we become vulnerable to changes dependant upon our environment.

The aim of living ayurvedically is to become harmonious to the environment around us. We do this by looking at ourselves and noting which element is going out of balance. Once identified, we can then begin our journey back to what I like to term 'yourself'. I also like to call this, 'coming home'.

The three doshas

In ayurveda, the constitutions are categorised according to the elements within them. The three main categories are called **doshas** and are termed vata, pitta and kapha.

Vata: If your prakruti has more of the elements of air and ether, you will be strongly in the vata constitution. You are very creative and free flowing. Your 'home' within yourself is also reflected in how you might keep your physical home - lots of colour, artistic items, maybe a little messy but full of energy and movement.

Pitta: If your prakruti contains more of the fire and water elements, your constitution will be more pitta. As such, you will be strongly placed in your intellect, your life will have focused order and you like to have things in control. Your physical home might be kept in the same way, with many books on the shelves and everything neat and in order.

Kapha: If you have more of the earth and water element in your constitution, you will be of the kapha dosha. You love to care for others, you are loyal and very grounded in nature. Your home will be cosy, warm and food will always be ready to be served.

Photo by Denis Oliveira

Balancing the elements

Balance is necessary for harmony, both within ourselves and outside of us. In ayurveda we understand that all of the elements require some nourishment and we have to look at all of them working as a synergy rather than isolating them from each other.

We can bring balance to our body – our internal home – with diet and herbs according to elemental qualities.

This concept of balance can be extended to our home environment by introducing new elements to balance our usual tendencies. For example, if our home is very pitta, we can add some softness and ease to it with more of the air and water elements. As such we can begin to understand the equilibrium with our external environment to reach balance.

The earth element

To acknowledge the presence of the earth element within our home we can keep many woody plants around, as well as crystals, special stones or rocks. The earth element also nourishes our sense of smell, which we can honour by using natural essential oils and burning incense. The earth element in a plant is the root and wood parts. You can keep this in mind when choosing plants for your home (for example, try to grow ginger - the method is on the following page).

The water element

This element has qualities of ease, flow and strength. We can introduce the water element by keeping very water dense plants in our home such as aloe vera and succulents (pictured below). Softer furnishings will also bring some gentleness and ease to the environment. Water is connected to our sense of taste, and so keeping a nice variety of food

Photo by Scott Webb

items in the home to bring flavour and taste is a good way to nourish this.

The fire element

Fire is an element with great importance in our lives. It governs transformation, clarity and action. When the season is dark, it is important to invite the fire element into our environment. We can do this very simply by lighting candles. Bringing light into your home this way can bring warmth and a space for processing. Fire is connected to our sense of sight. Trataka is a yogic practice that involves gazing into a candle flame. It is very cleansing for our eyes and also our mind. The fire part of a plant is colour, so brightly coloured flowers are a great way to introduce this element into the home.

The air element

Air is a vital part of life. Without our breath we cannot perform our bodily processes that require movement and communication. Regularly allow fresh air to flow into the home to reduce stagnancy and to keep the energy moving. Air is connected to the sense of touch. Have a variety of textures in your furnishings and plants. The leafy part of plants is the air element, and so include lots of leafy plants to encourage the element of air, and of course you can also add in some air plants *(see photo below)*.

The ether element

Ether is the subtle quality between air molecules. You can call it 'space' or nothingness. Space is very important for growth and expansion. We can bring aspects of this element into our home by simplifying our possessions and having an open area where we can sit and reflect. Ether is connected to our sense of hearing. Nourish this with pleasant sounds, so open the windows to hear morning bird song and listen to soothing music.

Photo by Naina Bajaria

Self care is like plant care

I have found that the qualities and necessities required for a plant to grow are similar to our own needs. Yet we sometimes fail to see this, despite taking good care of our plants! We can learn a lot from the way plants grow, requiring a careful balance of water, air, sunlight, nourishment and space.

When a plant requires more water, it appears dry. The same is true for us if we have the awareness to observe dryness in our body.

Most importantly, our plants need a home. They need a safe environment where they can adapt and grow. The same also goes for us. We, too, must find our own home within ourselves in order to flourish and grow to our fullest potential. For this we require awareness and understanding of our needs, much of which we can learn directly from the way that we take care of our plants.

Photo by Gaelle Marcel

Grow your own ginger

Ginger is a very common plant used in ayurvedic medicine. Add this lovely root to tea, soups and curries for a heating quality. A slice of fresh ginger with a pinch of rock salt and lime juice before meals is very beneficial for your digestion.

You can easily grow ginger at home starting from spring.

Photo by 'Alive Photo'

- Take shop bought ginger (try to get organic) and choose a piece with some nodules.
- Soak the piece in warm water overnight before planting.
- Plant the ginger with soil in a long shallow container with the nodules pointing upwards. Cover with 1-2 inches of soil then lightly water. Make sure the container has drainage.
- Water regularly and keep the pot out of direct sunlight. You should notice that shoots begin to form after 2-3 weeks. You can harvest the ginger after a few months. 🌿

MOON RITUALS

Jo Cauldrick illustrated the colouring sheets on the
following pages. Settle down with a cup of your
favourite herbal tea and enjoy colouring them in.

CLEANSE YOUR CRYSTALS

RELEASE YOUR DREAMS

RITUALS

FULL MOON

FILL A ROOM WITH CANDLES

TREAT YOURSELF TO A LOVELY MEAL

ENJOY THE MAGIC

WRITE ANYTHING YOU WANT TO LET GO OF & BURN IT

FULL MOON DOWN

BAKE A FULL MOON CAKE

BREATHE

Photo by Samuel Zeller

LOVE + CRYSTALS

"More love means healthier plants."

Crystal Whisperer, Katie-Jane Wright, shares her tips for showering your plants with love to help them thrive. Find out which crystals boost their growth and how we can connect with elemental energy.

Words and photos by Katie-Jane Wright

Plants and crystals go hand in hand – they complement each other perfectly energetically, they are both gifts from mother earth, and are grown in the ground. Plants and crystals have so many lessons to teach us.

These days my house is scattered with crystals and house plants, but I need to be honest with you: I never used to be very good at keeping plants alive. At times I can be scatty and forget to water them. I'm happy to say that things have changed – I connected to the energies around me and a new perspective opened up.

My grandmother was a wonderful Indian lady who healed with her hands: it is in my ancestry. She originated from the foothills of the Himalayas in a small Hill tribe in northern India. She was known for bringing plants back to life. Everyone knew that if they had a sick plant, they only had to hand it over to her and within days it would be flourishing and dripping with new flowers. Her secret? She could intuitively connect with a plant's energy – she spoke to them, sung to them and loved all over them. This sounds simple, and it really is. The loving energy you put into your plants makes their energy field resonate and they respond to your love by growing.

I watched a beautiful show recently where a Buddhist monk sung praise to the vegetables and plants that she grew. She let them grow where they wanted and only picked them when she *felt* they were ready to become an offering. Even the way she prepared and cooked them was a conscious, mindful meditation. The whole process was so beautiful and respectful. When we tune into a plant's energy it can help us go deeper into our heart and find elements of ourselves that we are missing. This takes us one step closer to being whole. As Albert Einstein said, *"Look deep into nature, and then you will understand everything better."*

I am a psychic and intuitive healer: I see, feel and hear energy. The way I communicate with my crystals is in a very open-hearted way. I simply ask them if they need to be cleansed. Crystals have subtle energy bodies that soak up frequencies around them. They are record keepers and hold all of the earth's secrets.

When you begin to connect with your plants, you will feel when they need feeding. You will sense when they need your attention. Always go with your first gut answer: this is your intuition.

In truth, I know that I was not blessed with my dear grandmother's talents for plants, but I have nurtured my understanding and love for the plant world. I now treat plants and flowers in a new way, by opening my heart to them. I shower them with vibrant pink light vibrations so we establish a connection. When you approach everything with love and lead from your heart, whether it is creating, writing or tending to a house plant, you are pouring that love into the very thing you are focusing on and they feel it. The thing that you created becomes attuned to your heart vibrations and it lifts it. If it's writing, you will feel the love through words. Your heart asks you to 'feel', not to think as much, but to trust it and follow it.

Plants are living organisms with an energetic system similar to ours. They have an aura like us, which is our energetic blueprint. It can be full of colour and changes with the seasons, emotions and moods.

I approach my care for plants as I would working with crystals. This is an approach that I feel can be applied to everything. Awareness is key: awareness of the self, of your energy and the way it ebs and flows through your body like tides rippling across a beach. I learnt to tune into my own energy by simply sitting silently and quieting my mind as best I can through meditation. I have found through much personal exploration, especially with trees, that we can gain their trust if we open our hearts fully to them.

Try this visualisation

I use this visualisation when connecting with the elemental energy of plants, trees, flowers, animals and crystals. It is not limited to one thing. In this instance I am going to connect with a tree, but you can do the same thing with smaller plants but perhaps don't place your hands on them if they are delicate.

1. Stand in front of the tree and place both hands on the bark, take a moment to breathe in deeply and take in the texture of the bark – the look and smell of it.

2. Now imagine an energy field around the tree, like a bubble. Start to breathe it in on the next inhale. Give it a colour, if that helps.

3. Slowly come back to your body and bring your focus and awareness to your heart where a pink rose rests. On each breath, open it petal by petal. Once it is open, really connect with your heart and all the love there – feel its warm pink glow.

4. Take that pink glow down from your heart, across your chest, down through your arms and out of your right hand.

5. Once you have opened your heart to a plant, it will feel your intention. You will have made a link with them and they will buzz with your energy. The proof is in how healthy they glow, how happy they feel, how much they flower and how fast they grow.

PLANTS ARE MAGIC #4 HOME

"THE LOVING ENERGY YOU PUT
INTO YOUR PLANTS MAKES
THEIR ENERGY FIELD RESONATE
AND THEY RESPOND TO YOUR
LOVE BY GROWING."

Add crystals into soil to boost plants

I would like to share with you my go-to crystals that I pop into the soil with plants to encourage growth, strength and protection. You can bury crystals in the soil or just pop them on the top. You can use a few or just one. I'll share my top four crystals that I like to use in soil, but remember - there is no right or wrong, so if you use other types of crystals that's fine. Above all, trust your intuition.

Rose quartz: *(pictured below)* If your plant is feeling down, droopy and wilting, give it some extra loving vibes with rose quartz. It's the stone of love, self care, compassion and forgiveness. It sends all these loving energies to the plant and its aura, and as you know - more love means healthier plants.

I like to use rose quartz aura in my ivy. This is rose quartz that has been alchemised at a high temperature with precious metals, so it shines a gorgeous iridescent glow. This stone has been keeping my plants alive and very happy. I find that with this energy, they flower bigger and last longer without water.

Moss Agate: This is my elemental stone. It has inclusions of manganese and iron which grow in similar patterns to moss and lichen. When you hold this stone up to the light you will see worlds within worlds. This is a fascinating stone and gives us slower, strengthening and grounding energy.

Throughout history, moss agate has been known as the crystal for gardeners and is recognised as offering benefits in agriculture. If you pop a piece in the soil, it promotes growth and overall health for your indoor plants, and is also useful outdoors – in vegetable and flower beds.

Clear quartz: This stone is a great accompaniment to any other stone. Clear quartz is a master healer, working to all energy centres. It's an amplifying stone that will double the energy of other stones that you pair it with. It's a great clearing and purifying stone, so pop it in with any plant that is sick or looking a bit sad.

Shungite: Shungite is a powerful stone of protection and transformation. Pockets were found in Russia two billion years ago when there was none or very little life on earth. It's composed of carbon. Carbon forms the building bricks of life and this is why shungite is known as the stone of life. It's the only stone known to contain fullerenes, which is a crystalline form of carbon full of antioxidants which have neutralising effects. Shungite works to protect against bacteria, fungus, and even harmful chemicals. It rescues and stimulates growth in plants (and us) and boosts and protects from harmful electromagnetic fields (EMFs) and other geopathic stress.

My local plant nursery has a 'Hospital zone'. It's a section at the back of the little family-run place where they tend to their sick plants. There's a little sign that reads: *"Sick plants. Please be quiet and try not to use your phone."* These guys are aware of energy and they know that these plants are in a restful state – their leaves have shed, they are damaged and need some peace and quiet to recover. I find the concept of plant energy being susceptible to the microwaves of phones interesting. We are affected by them too, so why shouldn't plants be? At home I try not to place my plants by any electrical equipment, but if I do then I pop a piece of shungite into the soil or close to the pot, which blocks against electromagnetic waves.

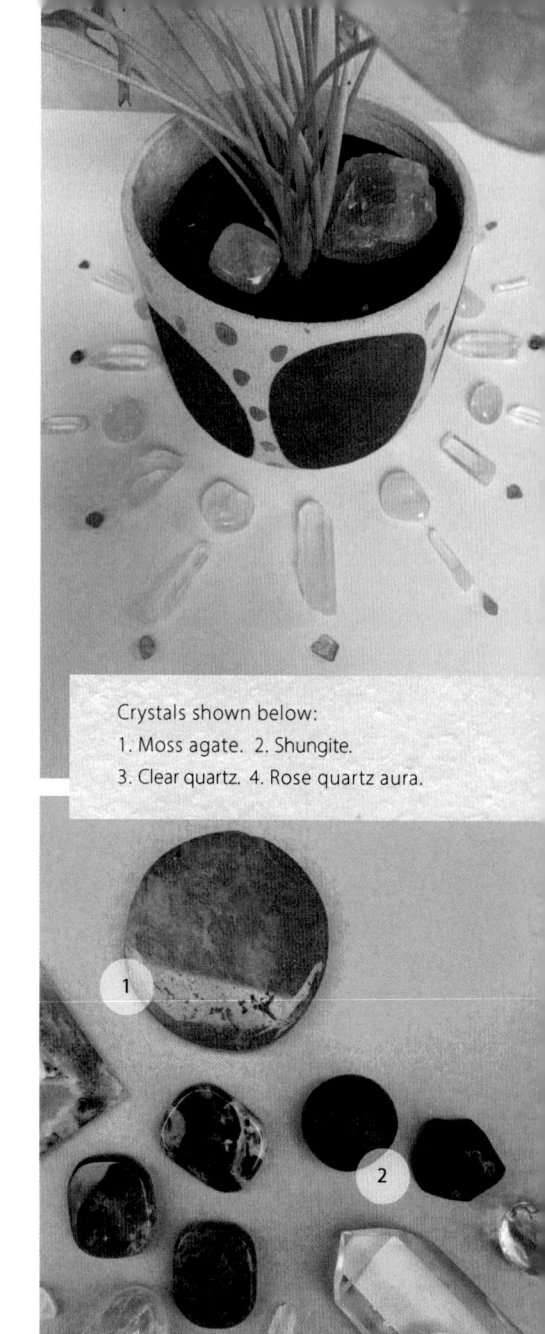

Crystals shown below:
1. Moss agate. 2. Shungite.
3. Clear quartz. 4. Rose quartz aura.

Crystal grids

Gridding plants with crystals is something that can be done to focus a specific intention and energy on them. I often grid my tea and water before I drink it. In fact you can grid and bless the water before you feed it to a plant, then you'll infuse it with loving vibrations, intentions and blessings. If you get into the practice of doing this, please do it for the water you drink too.

What you need

- Your plants - you can grid one or a group.
- At least 8 crystals. Tumble stones are inexpensive and it's always good to include some clear quartz points.

Set up your grid intuitively

Place the water or plant in the centre and build a grid of crystals around it. A good place to start is with some quartz points and a mixture of any of the crystals mentioned on the previous page. You will need an even number: 8 stones would be good, but 4 is OK too. If you're using stones with points then make sure you point these towards the plant.

Bind the grid

Once you have set up the grid, the most important part is to bind it with intention.

You can hold a clear quartz point in your left hand and do the exercises to open your heart (on page 68), and hold the intention in your heart and mind to infuse the plant with love, your heart's light and a boost of fresh energy. It depends what you would like to achieve as to what your intention is. For example if your plant is wilting and not looking healthy, you could bind the grid with free healing light.

Make sure you use the quartz point (or your hand, visualizing energy and light coming out of it) to connect each stone to the centre energetically. Work with each stone one at a time in a clockwise motion and return to the centre after each stone. Go back and forth connecting each stone to the other and looping back to the centre, almost like the pattern of a bicycle spoke. Continue until they are all connected with energy and light.

Take your gridding further

I have given you some basic tools for gridding your plants and also the water you feed them. There is a meditative art to constructing crystal grids which you can read more about in my book *Crystals: How to tap into your infinite potential through the healing power of crystals.* 🌿

GARDEN STORIES

"Feeling the land pulse underneath my bare feet and inside of my body reminds me of where I am and how I connect to this place. There is something very magical about this relationship."

Words and photos by Cat

Home is where you can name the birds after their song. Where the teapot simmers and your hand reaches for the jar of dried herbs without thinking. The soft corner your tired feet lead you and your closed eyes after a long day. The way the sun rays play with the dust through the window in swirls that tell stories only you can read.

Home is away from home. Home is a backpack full of clothes and a bar of soap. Home is the laughter of a stranger reminding you of your grandmother. It is a foreign land you have ties with, waking up from their slumber deep inside your bones. It is a plateful of your ancestral food that you've never seen before.

Home can be an object, or maybe it's a really small space. Maybe it isn't the space in itself, but what it holds. Home can be remembering too.

For me, part of home is where my garden

is. After moving homes a handful of times, I've come to realise that the places harder to leave are the ones where I had rooted. I root through plants. As my trees, vegetables, bushes and flowers spread their rhizomes down, so do I, figuratively. It is no coincidence that our ancestors abandoned their nomadic habits when agriculture was developed. To grow plants – specifically food – holds so much meaning to me. It symbolises not only a reciprocal relationship to the land, but a strong tie to our forebears as well.

Whenever I walk down to my garden to harvest something for a meal, I feel a wave of empowerment wash through my body. I feel connected to my grandmothers, and great grandmothers and so on, across different continents with very different climates, innate practitioners of self-reliance, carrying old knowledge, folk medicine and traditions. Today, in a world where everything is so readily available to us, people with the

privilege of location and means, I see the choice to steward land and grow food as very significant. It is even, I dare say, an act of *resistance* – against the corporate world that puts food on our plates, the market-driven ethos and issues behind large-scale food production, the capitalist logic that is incompatible with sustainability.

When it comes to my garden, I try to be intentional about what grows in there. Weeds and volunteer plants are welcome and part of a thriving ecosystem, and I like cultivating varieties that have a relationship to my bioregion, either by being indigenous to here or by having been grown locally for so many generations that they have become

"AS MY TREES, VEGETABLES, BUSHES AND FLOWERS SPREAD THEIR RHIZOMES DOWN, SO DO I, FIGURATIVELY."

heirlooms – adapted to our climate, resistant to pests, grown for flavour and quality and not for aesthetics or shelf life. Having these vegetables and fruits as part of my diet represents such a meaningful connection to the hills where I live.

A plant can hold so much – it's never just a plant. It tells stories of its evolution and adaptation, it speaks of its climate and pests and it holds tales of who grew it and how that came to be. Many of my seeds come from seed swaps within my community. This is a way of making sure we're reclaiming seed sovereignty and keeping locally-adapted varieties alive. It's a way of sharing our growing successes, keeping strong plants going, and passing around special and interesting-looking plants. After all, we all appreciate a vegetable that falls almost outside of our comfort zone popping up in between our zucchinis.

Bioregion, land, community, seed, plant, body. This connection is home too. Feeling the land pulse underneath my bare feet and inside of my body reminds me of where I am and how I connect to this place. There is something very magical about this relationship.

Today it is a full moon. I stayed outside, in my garden, with my eyes closed, listening to the sounds of an owl in the distance and to the gentle rustle of the oak leaves above my head, together singing a lullaby that translates something like this: "home".

GARDENING IS RESISTANCE

RESISTANCE IS FERTILE

Artwork and photos by Jai Bess
jaibirdpress.co.uk

LIVING COLOURS

Join us for a conversation with textile designer and natural dyer, Samorn Sanixay, who founded the weaving cooperative *Eastern Weft* in her birth country Laos, as a way of providing employment for women in the Hill tribes.

Photos by Samorn Sanixay and Eastern Weft

Hi Samorn. In the last issue of Plants Are Magic you shared a beautiful tutorial showing us how to hammer flowers ino cloth to create patterns. This opened our eyes to a whole new world of botanical dyeing. I'm so looking forward to talking to you again!

Can you tell us how you started dyeing with plants?

Although I've always had a passion for creating and making, my work as a textile designer came about from a completely different path in life.

At University I studied Political Science in Asian Studies with a Diploma in Japanese Language. In 2002, I had the opportunity to return to my birthplace of Laos where I joined UNICEF (United Nations International Children's Emergency Fund) as a consultant and translator. I can speak Lao, conversational Thai and basic French. I was also a script writer for children's books and cartoons based on health and education. We were given different topics to focus on, so we would do research and then write a story book based on factual evidence from our research.

We were sent to remote villages and in some of these villages there was no running water or electricity. After work there was not much to do so I would roam and talk to villagers. I always saw women weaving underneath their houses. I would go and sit and watch them and it started from there. I asked the villagers if I could learn and I was able to weave two metres of fabric on my

Above: Samorn. *Opposite:* Dyes made from eucalyptus leaves.

own and I made a skirt for myself.

That day redirected my course in life in many ways. It made me really reflect on my life and what a privileged upbringing I'd had compared to these girls in villages.

Can you tell us more about the weaving and dyeing in Laos?

In remote villages there is nowhere to buy supplies so everyone must make their own products and this usually means from scratch. Women weave cloth to clothe their families and keep them warm. It's real sustainable living out of necessity!

Young girls are taught to weave at a very young age by their mothers and grandmothers.

There are over 70 different ethnic minority groups in Laos and many of them live in remote parts in the mountains or jungles living a subsistence life. Each group has its own particular customs and clothing as a way of identity. For example in the south, bordering Cambodia, they grow and weave cotton on the back-strap loom and use homegrown dyes. In the north of Laos there are Hill tribes such as the Hmong and they produce skirts that are made from scratch using hemp, batik and indigo, with silver adornments and headpieces. In the north east, they have some of the most complex weaving techniques that exist in the world created by supplementary weft weaving.

"THE PLANTS USED FOR DYEING INCLUDE COCONUT HUSK FROM JUICE MAKERS AT THE MARKET, JACKFRUIT WOOD, MANGO LEAVES, SAPPAN WOOD..."

What are some of the plants you learnt to dye with?

There are so many! The plants used for dyeing are all local and seasonal. Examples are discarded coconut husk from juice makers at the market, jackfruit wood, mango leaves, indigo, marigold, tamarind leaves, sappan wood and leaves, annatto, teak leaves, rosella.

When your time in Laos came to an end, you set up a weaving house called Eastern Weft. Can you tell us a bit more about how you came to do this?

At the end of 2004 when my contract with UNICEF came to an end, I decided to start my own venture and continue to support young women and girls of ethnic minority Hill tribes. Eastern Weft was set up with my master and weaving instructor Khaisy.

I wanted to keep close links with Laos. It was my birthplace and seeing all the incredible different textile traditions that existed made me want to share this with the world.

The biggest motivation for setting up the weaving house was because the young people of ethnic Hill tribes are looked down upon and they cannot find work in the cities because there is stigma attached to Hill tribes. However, every single one of them has been taught weaving from their mothers since they could walk. Each tribe can be identified through their clothing and textiles. To me this was so fascinating and I wanted to share and translate stories through

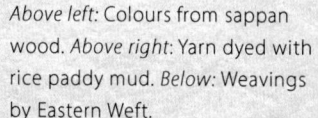

Above left: Colours from sappan wood. *Above right:* Yarn dyed with rice paddy mud. *Below:* Weavings by Eastern Weft.

Above: Marigold flowers.
Below: Ebony seed pods
(Diospyros Ebenum).

textiles. So with our collections we mix all the different techniques and this is rarely done between tribes.

In the weaving house, what kinds of plants are used for dyeing?

We use all the plants mentioned above and more including stick lac, ebony seed pods, rice paddy mud, tamarind fruit, mangosteen shell and pomegranate. Plus lots of different types of wood that we collect in the forest.

The way we dye and produce textiles always revolves around the seasons: 'local and seasonal' is part of our motto. We take what is discarded from nature, as well as waste from markets, such as coconut husks. We also dye with the marigold flowers after Buddhist rituals, lunar celebrations and prayers.

Your home is in Canberra, Australia. Can you tell us about the plants you grow in your garden?

Yes, I have an edible garden as well as a dyer's garden! I have almost twenty varieties of rose, Japanese maple, geranium, pansies and chrysanthemum. Then in my edible garden I have plants like sorrel, sage, several types of mint, as well as many other herbs, tomatoes, nasturtium, raspberries and blueberries.

You make incredible colours and patterns from food waste. What are some of your favourite fruits and vegetables to use?

I like all food waste from fruit and vegetables. My favourites are maybe

eggplant (aubergine) skin and the humble onion. These are things that most people regard as waste. I look at it as a creative challenge. I will try a plant once and if there is something in it then I will try another technique the next time.

Can you tell us about the dyeing you do when you travel and what these textiles mean to you?

Dyeing has become an 'intertwined' part of my life the last few years. Of course, I can't help but try leaves from trees I see when I'm on the road.

All the weavings and textiles that I've ever designed or produced tell stories of people and places and most importantly about our connection with nature. The shapes are inspired by plants and animals in tropical forests.

Last year I travelled with my children for about four months around Europe and Asia. I decided to collect colours and prints of plants from all the wonderful cities and towns that we visited. It was imprinted into cloth, literally. I called it my Travelling Scarf *(see the photo on the next page)*. It became very colourful and full of the flowers and plants that I hadn't seen before – from plants where I could see some colour or dye could be extracted from them.

I collected fallen flowers and walked down to the sea to find wild plants, a bit like the way a child searches for shells on the sand. I really enjoyed scouring and foraging to add to my scarf. I wouldn't leave a place without adding new colour. It was also a good conversation subject.

"THE WAY WE DYE AND PRODUCE TEXTILES ALWAYS REVOLVES AROUND THE SEASONS: 'LOCAL AND SEASONAL' IS PART OF OUR MOTTO."

Do you continue to discover new things from your experiments with plants?

Yes, even today there are plants that I have always overlooked because they are so common or I see every day that I don't think twice about them. Sometimes I accidentally brush past a plant and break a stem or branch, so I bring the branch home and then try to see if any colour can be extracted. Buddleja was a wonderful surprise; each technique produced different unexpected colours.

Another plant I haven't had interest in dyeing with until fairly recently is eucalyptus. I am surrounded by hundreds of trees that I ride or walk past each day. Many other people who work with

Above and opposite: Making dyes from food waste. *Below:* Samorn's 'Travelling Scarf' made by hammering flowers into silk.

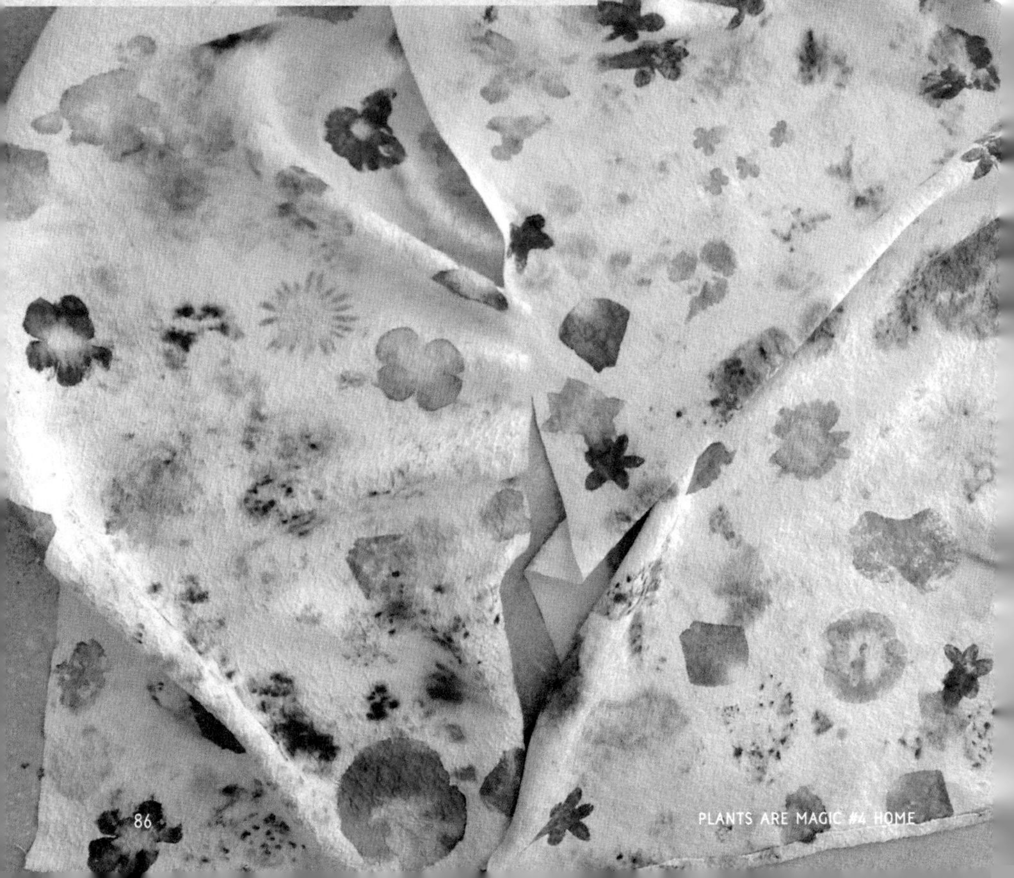

natural dyes focus solely on eucalyptus prints but that wasn't really my interest or area. Then when the council cut down several trees at the front of the street, I just had to bring branches home and experiment in my own way. Through this, I discovered that the possibility of colour never ends!

When you cook food, do you like to cook intuitively rather than follow recipes? Are cooking and dyeing closely linked for you?

My mother is illiterate so of course she could not read recipes and she was taught to cook by her mother. In Asia, cooking is mostly intuitive and by tasting what you are making and never following a recipe. That's the way I have learnt to cook and I suppose it follows me in my creative practice. I have a good sense of what I'm doing.

So, yes, cooking and dyeing are closely linked. Sometimes I bring work home and I'm dyeing something in the pot as well as making dinner. When I do this I make sure the dye is an edible one or food waste (like passionfruit, pomegranate skin or onion skin) so I don't poison my family or contaminate anything!

Cooking is also seen as a creative challenge so I don't get bored with the same meals. I am good at improvising and anything that goes wrong, I am almost always able to fix or save some part of it. I learnt that from my mother. She can fix and mend anything; she is a really industrious woman. This is all done out of necessity of course. However, some dinners I have burnt beyond charcoal!

Do you have a favourite plant that makes you feel most at home?

Yes, my favourites are two leaves that nearly everybody loves and knows.

Of Asian plants I would have to say mints. I like the smell of mint, it's fresh and brings back good memories of summer dishes as a child. It's a real palate cleanser.

Of western plants, it's sage. It has all the medicinal benefits and I adore the taste of sage in butter. I love the pattern it creates when you pound it on fabric. It's almost a treat. Most of all I love the colours: sage can be a greyish colour and when it flowers it's so beautiful. 🌿

To see more, visit *easternweft.com* and *instagram.com/samorn_sanixay*

DYEING WITH BERRIES

We can make a beautiful range of dye colours from berries. I'll show you how to turn your dyed fabric swatches into a mini patchwork lavender sachet, or you could dip dye your old clothes to give them a new lease of life.

Words and photos by Rebecca Desnos

1. Gather your equipment & materials

When we dye with entirely edible dye plants we can use kitchen equipment. For other dyes, always use separate tools.

What you need:

- A few large glass/china bowls
- Potato masher
- Sieve and muslin cloth for straining
- Stirring spoon
- 100% natural fabric, such as cotton or linen (I'm using an old white cotton sheet)
- Frozen edible berries of your choice. I've used raspberries and wild blueberries. Try edible berries that you grow in your garden, such as blackberry and blackcurrant.

How long will the colours last?

Berries are considered "stains" rather than true dyes and the colours are unlikely to last more than a couple of years. The bright shades gradually dull to muted shades of brown and grey. Nevertheless, we can still enjoy the beautiful hues while they last. Once your berry-dyed fabric or clothing has faded, simply dye it again.

2. Prepare your fabric

Choose your fabric and cut it to size. I'm using an old white cotton sheet that I've cut up into small pieces. Bare in mind that the more fabric you put into your dye, the lighter the shade will be and it may turn out mottled (which, in fact, can be quite beautiful!)

Wash your fabric with a natural laundry soap, then leave to dry or move onto the next step straight away.

Pretreat your fabric with almond milk

This is a variation of the 'soya milk method' from my book *Botanical Colour at your Fingertips* (2016). The protein in the milk coats the fibres and builds a layer of protein that acts as a bond between the dye and the fibre. Try experimenting with other types of milk too. You can skip the milk pretreatment, but your colours may turn out lighter and not last quite as long.

Buy organic almond milk (look for milk that contains only almonds and water), or make your own using the recipe below.

Almond milk recipe

- Soak half a cup of dried almonds in water over night.

- In the morning, discard the water and rinse the almonds. Peel off the outer skin.

- Put the almonds in a blender along with 2 cups of water and blend.

- Strain through a sieve lined with a muslin cloth (or a nut bag) and squeeze the pulp in the cloth to extract as much of the liquid as possible.

- Use the milk immediately or store in the fridge for up to 4 days.

Next we will dilute the milk and soak our fabric in the liquid

- Dilute the milk with cold water using the ratio of 1 part milk : 5 parts water. Pour the milk into a large bowl or bucket and add in the proportional amount of water.

- Dampen your fabric under the tap and drop it into the milk. Top up the level of water, if needed. This gives the fabric more space to soak.

- Keep it somewhere cool (even put it in the fridge, if you have the space) and allow it to soak for 12 hours. Stir it from time to time. After 12 hours, remove the fabric and squeeze out as much liquid as possible so it doesn't drip. You can put it in your washing machine on a spin, if you have that cycle. (Once you've taken the fabric out, put your machine on a rinse cycle to clean it). Allow the fabric to dry.

- Dip the dry fabric back into the liquid briefly so it receives another coating of milk. Squeeze out the liquid again. Then leave it to dry.

- Do one final brief dip, squeeze out the liquid and allow it to dry fully.

- Set your fabric aside for a few days. This gives the coating of milk time to bind to the fibres before you dye it.

3. Cold water berry dyeing

Have you taken berries out of the freezer and noticed that they easily stain your fingers as they defrost? When we freeze berries, the water inside the fruit expands and bursts through the cell structure. Frozen berries release their colour readily. To preserve the bright colours, we will dye the fabric in cold dye.

- Weigh your fabric and measure twice the weight of berries. Soak the frozen berries in a large bowl of cold water. As they begin to defrost, mash the berries with a potato masher to release the colour. Leave them to soak for a while longer. When you're happy with the depth of colour in the liquid, take a second bowl and strain the liquid through a sieve lined with a muslin cloth *(as pictured on page 89)*.

- Now take the milk-treated fabric and dampen it under the tap. Then squeeze it in your hands to remove the air to avoid air bubbles when it goes into the dye. Place the fabric in the dye bowl and stir with a spoon and allow it to move freely. Leave it to soak in the liquid for as long as you like and stir every so often. Twelve hours is a good starting point, or you can leave it for longer. Lift the fabric out of the dye to monitor the shade and decide if you'd like to leave it for longer.

- When you you're happy with the colour, take your fabric out of the dye and squeeze it to remove as much liquid as possible (so it doesn't drip and develop streaks) then hang to dry. Once dry, rinse out the excess colour.

TAP WATER   ACID   ALKALI

WILD BLUEBERRIES

RASPBERRIES

4. Play with the pH

The pigments that are responsible for the colours in berries are called anthocyanins and they are pH sensitive. The dyes will change colour depending on whether they come into contact with acids or alkalis.

The pH of the water that you use to rinse the dyed fabric will affect the resulting colour. To shift the final colour to a different shade, fill a bowl with water and dissolve either a little baking soda (alkali/basic) or add a squeeze of lemon juice or vinegar (acid). After you've rinsed out the excess dye under the tap, return the fabric to the bowl of pH-altered water and watch the colour change before your eyes.

You can also paint these 'pH modifiers' onto the dyed fabric. Squeeze a little lemon juice into a bowl and in a second bowl dissolve some baking soda in a small amount of tap water. Take two paint brushes (one for each pot) and paint the liquids onto the dry fabric and watch your colourful patterns emerge.

Berry-dyed clothing is likely to be affected by the pH of our sweat, so bare this in mind for clothing. Also, the colour of clothing may shift back and forth each time it is washed, so enjoy the colour changing magic.

5. Painting with berry juice

It really is as simple as it sounds!

- Make yourself some concentrated berry juice by allowing a handful of frozen berries to thaw out in a bowl (don't soak them in water this time). Once they have defrosted, mash them then strain the juice through a sieve lined with a muslin cloth.

- Alternatively, allow berries to defrost in a bowl and dip your paintbrush into the juice that collects in the bowl *(as shown in the photo below)*.

- Use this berry juice to paint on cloth, then heat-set the dye with a hot iron. Some colours from berries will last longer than others. Try to wait a few days before rinsing the fabric, to give the dye the best chance of lasting.

- Try using the berry dye like watercolour paint on paper.

- If you'd like to keep the berry paint for a few days, store in a jar with a lid and add some salt and a few cloves. This will help the juice stay fresher for longer. Label it clearly so others know that it's paint and not food!

6. Make a mini patchwork lavender sachet

As I was dyeing fabric in different shades of lilac, I found myself dreaming about lavender. It felt so natural to sew these swatches into a mini patchwork, which I then turned into a little bag and filled it with dried lavender. These make lovely gifts. Just remember that berry dyes don't last forever, so the colours will gradually fade. But that's OK, since the scent of the lavender will gradually fade too. When the lifespan of your lavender pouch has come to an end, simply compost it.

Here are some simple steps for making your own lavender sachet:

- Cut up your fabric into different shapes and hand stitch them together with a back stitch.

- Once you've made a square or rectangle and are happy with the size, cut another piece of fabric the same size. This will be the back of your little quilt.

- Stitch the pieces together around the edges, with right sides facing, and leave a small gap on one side (big enough to turn the pouch around).

- Turn the pouch back the other way so the right sides are now on the outside, then fill with dried lavender. Slip stitch the open edge.

ZERO WASTE

We chat to Julia Watkins about creating less waste and how limiting our resources can ignite our creativity. Julia shares a few of her favourite recipes.

You started your zero-waste journey quite suddenly. What made you try it in the first place?

About four years ago I stumbled upon the book *Zero Waste Home* by Bea Johnson. I was completely taken by her book and moved by a You Tube video I watched of her shopping with reusable bags and glass jars.

My husband and I had worked in the environmental field our entire adult lives, so we were aware of conservation and climate issues, but we weren't necessarily living in a way that reflected what we knew and valued.

After reading *Zero Waste Home*, I slowly started to make changes, primarily by shopping at local farmers markets and using dry bulk bins to avoid packaged foods. I also started using cloth shopping, produce and bulk bags.

I carried on that way for a few years without making any other major changes. Then last year, when I was on a health kick and doing a juice cleanse, I

noticed that my refrigerator looked like Bea Johnson's! It was stocked almost entirely with fresh veggies and fruits, with nary a processed or packaged food in sight. As I stood there, admiring it, I took a photo and decided I was going to try going zero-waste. To document it visually, I created my Instagram account @simply.living.well.

What were some of the next changes you made?

After transitioning to using reusable produce and bulk bags, I started buying "wet" goods like vinegar, peanut butter, shampoo and conditioner in bulk at our local food co-op. I also began making my own cleaning supplies and toiletries. I made composting a priority.

Has it encouraged you to grow more food yourself?

Yes, definitely. I became much more intentional about buying and eating unpackaged, seasonal, and locally grown foods and, although I'll always support our local farmers market, I can't think of

a better way to eat locally than to grow your own food. Last year, I set up a small kitchen garden. It feels like an extension of my refrigerator and spice cabinet. I can't tell you the joy of being in the middle of making a meal, realising I don't have an ingredient and skipping out back to get it!

Has your relationship with nature developed since growing more of your own food?

Absolutely! Growing my own food keeps me connected to the seasons and the flora and fauna around me in such a heightened way. Last year, after I put in my garden, I started to notice which species of birds visited our yard, when they came, and what seeds they liked to eat. I noticed the bees, which flowers they were drawn to, and which plants they did and didn't pollinate. I noticed butterflies and the flowers they gravitated to, which helped me to plan a butterfly garden and waystation for the following spring. I watched the flowers the way one would listen to an orchestra, with certain species popping up in succession, one after the other. I absolutely love observing the rhythm of nature.

Have you learned some unexpected things along the way?

Oh, yes! Originally, my goal was to produce zero waste, as in absolutely no trash and eventually no recycling. I saw photos of people who could fit five years' worth of trash in a pint-size jar and set my sights on doing the same. Now, a year in, I understand that producing zero trash is extremely challenging, and not just because it's a lot of work to avoid packaging, but also because our economy is designed for waste. We live in a linear economy, where things are created around the principle of take, make, consume, and dispose, which puts the onus for reducing waste on the consumer instead of the producer.

We need a more sustainable model, specifically a circular one where products are designed around the principle of take, make, use, reuse, re-use again, and again, and again. Until then, I think we can only do our best and strive to produce less waste in our own unique ways. For me, that's meant taking inspiration from my grandparents and living more simply and slowly, growing some of my own foods, making foods

98

from scratch, using simple ingredients for cleaning, relying on old folk remedies for minor ailments, buying a lot less and secondhand when I do, owning only a few good quality things and taking care of them, repairing and mending things when they break, etc.

Do you enjoy the creative challenge?

I've always been a bit of a maker, but I've found that being slightly limited in terms of what resources I'm willing and able to use really stirs up the creative juices. For example, when you know your child loves to paint, but you don't want to go out and buy plastic tubes of paint you're left scheming up all sorts of possibilities. I'm currently making paint out of plant-based foods I can scrounge up from our fridge and spice cabinet. In the past, I'm sure I would have found an easier but much less creative way!

What was the most surprising thing that you've ever created?

I'd say it was laundry soap that I made from horse chestnuts I found in a neighbour's front yard. I had been inspired by your botanical dye book *(Botanical Colour at your Fingertips)* and started dyeing with plants from my backyard and neighbourhood. I brought home these huge conkers one day, curious to see what colour they would make, and discovered that in addition to making a pink-peach dye, they also made bubbles! Next thing I knew, I was researching and creating soap nuts for our laundry. It was such an exhilarating discovery to make – I honestly felt like crying as it was unfolding!

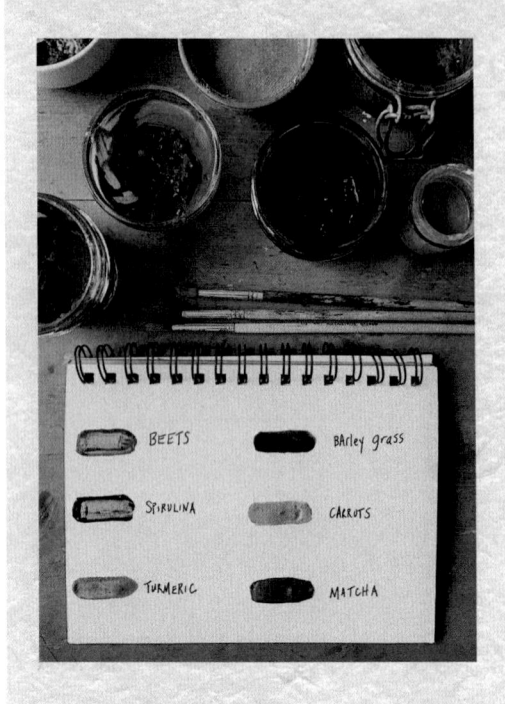

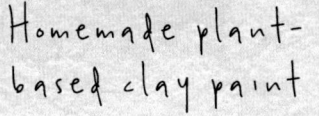

Homemade plant-based clay paint

Make your own naturally-coloured paints with ground spices and other edible powders, as well as beets and carrots (dehydrate these first then grind into a powder in a food processor or coffee grinder).

Mix the coloured powders with a small amount of powdered clay (such as bentonite or French clay) , which acts as a binder, then add in a spoonful of water at a time. Mix well, then add more water until you reach a pasty consistency.

These paints are fun for children and adults who like to experiment. Keep in the fridge for a couple of days.

Carrot top pesto

If there's one thing I love more than basil pesto, it's pesto made from food scraps that would normally be composted and never given the time of day. Those spindly greens on top of carrots can be used to make a pesto that is every bit as delicious as the one made from tender basil leaves.

To make the pesto:

1 cup of carrot top greens
¼ cup of pistachios
2 garlic cloves
2 tbsp fresh squeezed lemon juice
3 tbsp extra virgin olive oil
½ avocado (optional)
salt and pepper

Add the first four ingredients to a high speed blender or food processor. Blend until a chunky paste forms. You may need to stop occasionally to scrape down the sides. Add olive oil one tablespoon at a time until combined. If you want to make the pesto creamier, add the avocado and blend until a creamy paste forms. Add salt and pepper to taste.

Serve fresh with veggies, over pasta, on bread or crackers or store in the refrigerator in an airtight container for 3-4 days.

Citrus-infused all purpose cleaner

This citrus cleaner is such a simple and pure way to clean your home. Making it is as easy as infusing citrus food scraps in a jar of vinegar! If I were ever forced to turn in all but one of my homemade cleaning products, this would be the keeper.

To make the cleaner:

Gather 8-12 citrus peels (lemon, lime, orange, or grapefruit) and 2+ cups of vinegar (apple cider or distilled).

Add the citrus peels to a large glass jar and cover with vinegar. Cap with a tight-fitting lid or a cloth and rubber

band. If using a metal lid, place a piece of parchment paper between the jar and lid to prevent corrosion.

Set the jar in a sunny spot to infuse for two weeks. Afterwards, strain and compost the citrus peels, then pour the infused vinegar into a clean glass jar. When ready to use, dilute one-part vinegar to one-part water, add to a spray bottle, and use as you would any commercial all-purpose cleaner.

Since vinegar is acidic, it can damage certain surfaces and should not be used on natural stone. It can also strip the finish off of hardwood floors. That said, it can be used safely to clean just about everything else – windows, toilets, sinks and appliances.

PIGMENTS FROM PLANTS

Jule Kebelmann shows us how to extract dye from plants and make our own paint. Use the paint on paper or to decorate walls. This is a beautiful way to bring the qualities of your local plants into your home.

Words and photos by
Jule Kebelmann

I'm a textile designer with a love for herbs, plants and natural fibres. I brought these passions together in my business *Hey Mama Wolf*. We make local and sustainable knitting yarns and use only natural dyes. Painting the walls of our house in plant paints is another way for me to explore nature. Before I show you how to make these paints, let me tell you how I came to this idea.

A few years ago, my family and I moved from the centre of Berlin to the middle of nowhere, halfway to Hamburg. We were lucky to find an old water mill.

The house, which is about 250 years old, is in a general good shape thanks to its builders. Back then all the building materials came from the surroundings: boulders, stones, chalk, lime and clay from the fields, willow branches, oak trunks with wooden joints in the wooden

framework, mudbricks and sand. If it wasn't for the electrical lines and the 1970s plumbing, this ensemble of buildings would be fully compostable.

It still needs serious renovation and rebuilding. We (my man, two children and me) are doing most of the work ourselves and we make conscious choices and try to use local materials wherever possible. In three years we've finished just two rooms: the children's rooms. We're just about to begin working on our bedroom. We both work full time and have two small children so this is just the pace we have to accept. We truly embrace slowness and continue to live on a construction site!

Most of the walls are in plain chalk white but the natural clay colour is also quite lovely – it is warm and earthy so we will keep some of the walls in their natural

state. My son had the idea for a 'golden' wall. We painted it with mica (a naturally occurring silicate) and vegetable casein as binder directly on the brown clay wall. This brought me to the idea of painting walls with plant pigments. I did a bit of research and discovered that I had everything to hand to make lake pigments and began experimenting.

What is a lake pigment?

A lake pigment is a dye combined with an inert binder (e.g. a metallic salt) to make the dye insoluble in water. We will first extract dye from plants, then combine the dye with a metallic salt in a specific way to make a lake. A dye can be dissolved in water, but a lake pigment is insoluble in water and colours materials by dispersion. The technique I use to make lakes involves alum (an aluminium salt) and an alkali like washing soda.

Which plants can we use?

You can try this technique with any plant *(see safety notes on the opposite page)* that you can extract dye from. So far I have used avocado pits, coreopsis flowers, cherry tree bark, nettle, delphinium flowers, elder tree bark and mugwort.

Depending on the plants you use, the colourfastness will vary. In general the light fastness is not very high, but nevertheless, the paints still bring the characteristics of the plants into the home.

Tools + Ingredients

- Large pots and glass bowls
- Spoons for stirring and measuring
- Funnel
- Coffee filters
- Tray
- Cloth
- Pestle and mortar
- Brushes

- Plant matter and water
- Alum (potassium aluminium sulphate)
- Washing soda
- Acacia gum (gum arabic)
- Vegetable casein (legumin)
- Ammonium carbonate

Safety: Take care when identifying plants and ensure they are non-toxic. Use your own judgment when following the methods to ensure your safety. Wear a mask and safety glasses/goggles when working with powders. Wear an apron and gloves to protect your skin and clothes from powders, dyes and pigments. Don't inhale fumes from dye pots. When working with chemicals, please follow the safety instructions on the box or packet. Once you've used any equipment for dyeing, don't use it in the kitchen again. Work somewhere with good air circulation, away from children and animals.

1. Make the dye

- Gather your fresh or dried plant matter. Put it in a large enough pot and cover with water. We don't need as much water as for dyeing fabric or yarn because we want to make a strong solution. Let it sit overnight.

- The next day simmer it for 1-3 hours to extract the dye.

- Allow it to cool down or let it sit again over night. Then strain through a muslin cloth.

Optional

- To make different hues from the same plant matter you can use iron vinegar or copper vinegar solutions at the beginning of the process. These will shift the colour of your dye liquid. In general, iron will make the dye darker and copper will enhance yellows.

- Make your metal vinegars by soaking iron or copper pieces in vinegar and leaving them for a few weeks. Strain off the liquid and use to shift the colour of your dye.

2. Add alum

- Next we'll add alum to our dye liquid. Measure the volume of dye and make a note of this.

- For every 100 ml dye, prepare 5 tsp of alum solution. To make the alum solution, alum needs to be dissolved in boiling water in this ratio: 5 tsp of alum to 5 tsp of boiling water. Set this aside.

- Heat your dye solution to a simmer, then add 5 tsp of alum solution per 100 ml of your dye. This is a rule of thumb and stronger dye solutions may require more alum.

3. Add washing soda

- Choose a big enough pot to continue because it will get bubbly and foamy.

- Dissolve 1 tbsp of washing soda in half a cup of water. Add this alkaline solution drop by drop. Your dye should start to build foam. Stir, then stop adding the washing soda when it is all foamy.

- Let it sit, but stir from time to time.

- Once the foam has completely vanished (which may take some time), let the solution sit for a while longer to allow the sediment to fall to the bottom. It's handy to do this in a glass container so you can see the layer of sediment form. When the solution has built a sediment at the bottom you can carefully spoon off the liquid on top.

- Sometimes this clearer liquid still has enough colour, so be prepared for some amazements here! If it appears to be full of colour, reuse this liquid in steps 2 and 3 to make another batch.

4. Filter

- Now prepare a container with a funnel lined with a coffee filter. Strain the sedimented liquid through the filter. It will take a while to drip through and you can add more liquid until the filter is truly full.

- Then remove the filter carefully from the funnel. Open it on one side and lay flat on a prepared tray covered with cloth (these will get stained!).

- Spread the wet pigment on the filter and put it in a warm place without much direct light. Allow it to dry fully.

- Once dry, crack the pigment off the filter paper into a mortar. Break it up really well with the pestle: the smaller the particles, the better. You can also use a coffee grinder to get a really fine powder, but do not use it for food preparation again.

Lake pigment made from elder bark and iron

5. Make the paint

Now that you have your pigment, you can make paint. Here are two methods:

- The simplest way is to dissolve 1 part gum arabic powder in 2 parts water (or use liquid gum arabic). Then add the lake pigment and mix until you have a satisfying texture to paint with.

- Another method is to make paint with ammonium casein. I used vegetable casein that has added soda already within it. Use a big enough pot as it will get foamy again. Dissolve 4 tbsp casein in 8 tbsp cold water and allow it to stand over night. On the next day dissolve 1 - 1 ½ tsp ammonium carbonate in 6 tbsp warm (not hot!) water and add it to the casein.

Let it stand for about an hour and stir from time to time. When it's a uniform compound, it's done. Take your lake pigment and add to the ammonium casein until you have a rich coloured paste.

6. Let's paint

- Now you can paint your walls or make a painting on paper. If you have white chalk walls like I do, try first painting a layer of casein to seal in the wall. The chalk is water-soluble and will otherwise lighten your colour. 🌿

Futher reading

- Nick Neddo, The Organic Artist, Quarry Books.
- Helena Arendt, Werkstatt Pflanzenfarben, AT Verlag.

CORCOPSIS +
FARBERKAMILLE
aus dem Garten 16
PIGMENT - LACK
+ 42 Arkidung
NaSODA /18

AVOCADO-STEINE
ABGEKOCHT +
FRISCH
1. ABKOCHUNG
ALAUN + NATRON
/12
/17

BEEFUR
PIGMENT-LACK
AL + Soda
07.18

Thanks for joining us!

Let's keep in touch...

Join the mailing list
for musings on plants, creativity & simplicity.
www.rebeccadesnos.com/newsletter

Follow me on Instagram:
@rebeccadesnos / @plants_are_magic

Send an email:
info@rebeccadesnos.com

Portrait by Siobhan Watts

Other publications by Rebecca Desnos

Learn the art of *botanical dyeing*

Order past issues of *Plants Are Magic* magazine

www.rebeccadesnos.com

Plants Are Magic is an independent magazine for makers, dreamers & plant lovers.

Editor, creative director & publisher:
REBECCA DESNOS

web: www.rebeccadesnos.com
email: info@rebeccadesnos.com

Instagram: @rebeccadesnos /
@plants_are_magic

Front & back cover photos by Rebecca Desnos
Photo on page 1 by Annie Spratt

Logo by Inge van Geem

ISBN 978-0-9955566-4-5 (print)
ISSN 2514-2151 (digital)

Published by Rebecca Desnos
August 2019, in the UK.

Photo by Niklas Veenhuis